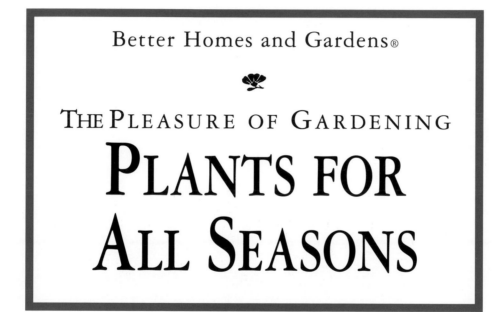

Better Homes and Gardens®

THE PLEASURE OF GARDENING

PLANTS FOR ALL SEASONS

Better Homes and Gardens®

THE PLEASURE OF GARDENING

PLANTS FOR ALL SEASONS

BY MARY MOODY

Better Homes and Gardens® Books

Des Moines

CONTENTS

THE LOVE OF
GARDENING

Introduction

There are many kinds of gardeners: those who spend every waking moment puttering; those who garden with great bursts of energy when time permits; those who have a strict routine for maintaining an orderly landscape, and those who sit and dream of what could be.

Like many enthusiasts, I never seem to have as much time with my hands in the soil as I would like. The pressures of daily life often keep me indoors, yet I still manage to maintain a garden that is enjoyed by many. It would be easy, of course, to employ a gardener to take over the routine chores, but somehow this would detract from the pleasure of knowing that every bulb planted has been personally blessed. So, by circumstance, I am a gardener who works in fits and starts, when time, energy and other commitments allow. As a result, I treasure every moment out of doors, and long for the day when I can garden at leisure, whenever I please.

So what is the pleasure of gardening? Why have flowers and gardens captured our hearts and minds since Egyptian times? (The temple gardens of Thebes were established as early as 1475 BC.) This fascination with plant life and gardens has been a continuous theme throughout literature and art in most cultures and civilizations, as demonstrated first in farming, and then showing itself in ornamental horticulture. The evolution of gardening in Greek and Roman times is well recorded in poetry, painting and writings that all show clearly a love of nature, both wild and tamed.

Initially, it is this love of nature that makes people feel an affinity for plants. Then a deep satisfaction emerges from the task of cultivation—the pleasure of watching a seed you have sown rise from the ground, flourish and flower. In the case of growing vegetables or herbs, the satisfaction is extended to the harvesting of the crops, then their preparation for the table. This is an age-old ritual, and one which I hope will always continue to bring joy in spite of modern mass farming production and supermarkets.

As a city person, born and bred, who now revels in the pace of semi-rural life, discovering how to grow things has been an adventure for me. When I was a child I spent long holidays in the country, where the sounds and smells of nature made a lasting impression. It wasn't surprising, therefore, that when the opportunity arose to escape the city I seized upon it, and have never looked back. There is something essentially satisfying about being in touch with the soil, being able to increase its fertility to the point where it can support healthy plant life. My family refers to me as 'the peasant' when I drool over a delivery of well-aged manure that has arrived for the mulching of the garden. The richness, texture and smell of this organic matter gives me great pleasure, a pleasure that non-gardeners find hard to comprehend.

BECOMING A GARDENER

Just as a garden evolves through the seasons and through the years, so too does the gardener's storehouse of knowledge and experience. Mistakes are often made, even after years of trial and error, but these are accepted as part of the process. As for the 'rules' of gardening, these are surely made to be broken. How often have I heard a gardener complaining that a certain species 'simply won't grow' in his or her particular area, only to walk

LEFT: Clever arrangement of plants can be used as a device to lead the eye to a distant vista, or to frame a view. Here an edged pathway of catnip (Nepeta sp.) creates a cloud of color, covered by archways of climbing roses including the spectacular rosa 'Joseph's Coat', with multi-colored red and yellow blooms. The deep green of the conifer hedge provides a solid backdrop.

PREVIOUS PAGE: This very natural looking pergola is at Ashtree Cottage in Wiltshire. Punctuated by golden honeysuckle, the pinks and blues planted below include delphiniums and two roses, 'Comte de Chambord' and 'Veilchenblau'.

around the corner and discover that same plant thriving! Virtually all things are possible, and a sense of adventure must be developed if something original is to be achieved. Like most creative arts, gardening is derivative, yet there is tremendous scope for individual expression in garden design. No two gardens are ever exactly alike, and each must therefore express something of the creative talent of the gardeners involved.

In my growing awareness of all things horticultural, I have been greatly affected by certain gardens I have visited, or by those I have read about and seen in books penned by like-minded enthusiasts. Not surprisingly, my tastes have changed dramatically in the last 15 years as my appreciation of the art of gardening has evolved. General tastes in garden design have changed too, with a renewed interest in the 'cottage' style of gardening—heritage roses, perennial beds and borders, box-hedges and classical Italian-style courtyards are again in vogue. Books that glorify the designs of gardeners such as Vita Sackville-West, Gertrude Jekyll and Edna Walling clearly demonstrate this leaning. Their use of color and texture in the landscape is without parallel, as is their innate sense of how

LEFT: A blue and white theme in classic cottage style. Tall spikes of delphinium 'Summer Skies' in a delightful shade of soft sky blue with white centers, are staked to prevent the heavily-laden flower spikes from wind damage. The clear white blooms of the floribunda rose rosa 'Iceberg' are offset by the large trumpet flowers of the regal lily (Lilium regale) which are tinged with pink.

plants are best combined. The cottage gardens of rural England, the fragrant vegetable and rose gardens of the South of France, the formal parterre gardens of Tuscany, the romantic régence gardens of Holland, and the exquisite spring blossom gardens of Japan all contain elements that have inspired both myself and many others who share this mutual respect for the artistry in gardening.

Over the past century the movement of people around the world has accelerated, hastened even more by the advent of speedy international travel. Indeed, since as far back as the fourteenth century human travel has been responsible for the distribution of plant species from one environment to another, to the point where truly 'native' gardens are now rare indeed. Roses, which were only ever found growing wild in the northern hemisphere, are now to be found thriving in every corner of the globe. Two centuries ago the roses of Europe flowered in one short flush each year, until the recurrent flowering roses of China were brought to the west, revolutionizing the breeding of the genus. It is this repeat flowering habit that has made the rose the world's most popular flowering plant, with breeders in many countries developing new hybrids every season.

In this respect gardens have shaken off their regional limitations. The eucalypts of Australia are seen thriving in California and the South of France; the proteas of South Africa are cultivated in the United States, New Zealand, and Europe, and tulips bred in the Netherlands are grown in most countries, as are South American jungle cacti and Asian

carnivorous species such as *Nepenthes* (pitcher plant). This cross-fertilization of species from one country to another has not come without its problems, as some varieties have so rapidly adapted to their new environment that they have overwhelmed the local flora, causing concern among environmentalists. The movement of plant life has also caused the transference of certain pests and diseases from one continent to another, and this has resulted in quarantine laws becoming more rigid in certain countries. Yet, despite these restrictions, wherever you travel and visit gardens you will see plants from a tremendously wide range of sources.

In gardening the possibilities and the choices are endless; so diverse is the subject that even experienced gardeners can be overwhelmed by the range of plants available, and the ways in which they can be incorporated into the landscape. My aims in writing this book are to share some of the joy experienced in planning and planting a garden; to inspire each gardener with confidence to use his or her own judgment; and to make easier those difficult decisions about how various plants can be best used, both for aesthetic impact as well as the more mundane practical considerations.

The gardening year has been divided into seasons so that readers will get a feeling for the rhythm of the working routine of a gardener, and an appreciation of the changing requirements of plants at various times of the year. *Plants for All Seasons* will help gardeners plan seasonal beds and borders, and learn more about the unique character of various species.

PRACTICAL
PLANT
SELECTION

Painting with Flowers

The best gardens are composed of a succession of scenes, or pictures, which are seen and enjoyed from different viewpoints. It is extravagant to plan your garden so that it flowers all at once, in one great blaze of color. Although spectacular, this burst will be short lived and will leave the landscape barren for the rest of the year, unless flowering annuals are planted in succession to bridge the gaps. The most successful gardens are planned to contain plants that will give some form of display at various times of the year. And 'display' does not necessarily mean flowers: it can refer to foliage in autumn, berries in winter or blossoms in spring.

First-time gardeners are often tempted to try to achieve a great deal in a short space of time, forgetting that the effect is

LEFT: A mixed flowerbed that demonstrates how well various plants work together, combining flower and foliage colors and textures, as well as height. The bright red flower spikes of the hollyhock (Alcea rosea) draw the eye to the center of the garden, softened by a blend of annuals, perennials and bulbs including lilies, poppies and catnip.

PREVIOUS PAGE: The charm of hollyhocks (Alcea rosea) in a massed planting, with tall spikes of rosette-like flowers in many colors. These cool-climate biennials (or short-lived perennials) are grown from seed planted in spring or autumn, and may need support as the flowerheads mature.

often best when allowed to evolve at a slow and steady pace. It is far better to work on one section, one scene, at a time, and feel comfortable that it has 'settled into the landscape' before moving on to another area of the garden. Another common mistake that is born of this early enthusiasm is visiting a nursery and buying a number of plants without first preparing beds or working out the best possible location for each species. As container-grown nursery plants need to be transplanted into the garden as soon as possible after purchase, this can lead to a frenzy of planting with little thought for the grouping of plants and the end result.

When considering your garden as a painting, think of the land as the canvas; think of the plants as the paints. Now, instead of assessing each plant as an individual entity, think of it in relation to the canvas and to the other elements of the scene. At first most of us look at plants for their individual appeal—their color, their texture, their fragrance—without thinking ahead to the next step of how that plant will combine, visually and in a practical sense, with the other plants in the garden.

A great deal depends on plain common sense. Plants with similar needs and requirements are best grouped together for obvious reasons. Apart from climate, considerations such the soil's pH level will strongly determine just what can

and can't be grown in a particular situation. Trying to combine plants with vastly different requirements will seldom succeed, although they will sometimes survive if the pH is fairly neutral, and an appropriate balance of nutrients is applied at the drip line (where the plant roots end, which is roughly in alignment with the tips of the branches). In the following chapter, 'Plant Associations', I have detailed plants that have similar requirements in terms of soil acidity/alkalinity as well as soil texture and drainage (they may, for example, need a sandy or clay soil), and the ability to withstand adverse conditions. Planting together plants with these common needs is vital if they are to produce the required results—although, of course, the rules can be bent a little at times.

With care it is possible to create a garden micro-climate that will enable a much wider range of plants to be cultivated. High garden walls or dense hedges used as windbreaks will prevent the garden from being battered by prevailing winds, and often raise the garden temperature. Masonry walls, in particular, are useful because they absorb heat from the sun and make the entire area much warmer. For example, despite living in a cold climate I have managed to grow tomatoes very rapidly indeed by planting them against a brick wall, which acts as a suntrap. The same principle applies to shrubs and perennials, which benefit from the stored heat, although they may need additional watering in summer if conditions are really hot.

It is also quite feasible to modify the soil to make it suitable for a wider group of plants. Both sandy and clay soils benefit greatly from the addition of well-aged composts and manures, either incorporated in the soil or used as mulch. This will greatly improve both the texture and drainage of the soil and therefore make it suitable for plants that it otherwise simply could not sustain. Likewise, where plants are to be grown intensively, additional nutrients and moisture will be required. Overcrowding of plants leads to a deterioration of quality, yet it can be done to some extent if the soil is sufficiently rich and moist.

SHOPPING FOR PLANTS

When shopping for plants, consider the following factors.

THE 'STYLE' OF THE GARDEN

This is sometimes determined by the architecture of the house itself. Traditional homes favor formal or cottage gardens, whereas more modern architecture calls for informal woodland or native landscapes. Artistic gardeners generally avoid the confines of a particular style, blending exotic and native species

together in an expression of their individual creative style. Simple garden styles are based on the tree, shrub and lawn combination (low maintenance), while more elaborate gardens feature roses, perennials, climbers and annuals in large cultivated beds (labor intensive).

CLIMATE CONDITIONS

Select plants that grow in your particular climate, while keeping in mind that certain plants will do well outside of their usual zones if the right 'immediate' conditions are provided, as described above. Local nurseries are usually careful to choose and breed stock that is suitable for the local area; unfortunately, supermarkets sometimes buy plants in bulk, and consequently sell varieties that are not ideal for the local climate zone. Species grown in the wrong climate may sometimes die (this may happen to frost-tender or sub-tropical species grown in a cool to cold climate when exposed to late spring frosts). Even if they survive, they will struggle along and be more prone to insect and disease attack because of the unfavorable growing environment.

AVAILABLE SPACE

Don't attempt to plant an oak tree in a small city courtyard garden, as it will be completely out of scale with the location and environment. Selecting the right plants for each situation will

RIGHT: The use of silver or gray foliage plants such as senecio and santolina throughout beds and borders creates an eye-pleasing contrast to basic green. Here a pink and yellow color scheme is softened by the silver-grays, combining pink hydrangeas, rock rose (cistus 'Silver Pink') in pink with yellow centers, and Santolina virens, *with bright yellow button flowers.*

depend largely on how much ground and climbing space is available. In a spacious country garden there is scope to experiment with larger-growing trees and shrubs, while in a city garden the possibilities will be determined by factors such as interference with neighboring properties and overhead or underground powerlines. Double-check the mature height and spread of plants before purchase, to ensure that your garden can realistically accommodate them when fully grown.

THE SOIL

Unfortunately, not all gardens are blessed with perfect soil conditions, and imperfect conditions restrict your scope with the variety of plants that can be cultivated. The quality of soil depends on the texture, drainage, pH balance and nutrient content. First-time gardeners should attempt to evaluate the soil before buying plants, as some remedial action may be necessary to bring the soil up to a level suitable for healthy cultivation.

When examining soil, consider the following factors.

Soil Texture

This will fall into one of three major categories: light and sandy; balanced, friable loam; and heavy and clay.

Light soil tends to crumble easily, sometimes forming a hard crust on the surface. It contains plenty of air, but moisture drains away quickly after rain or watering.

Clay soil is dense and slippery when wet, with little opportunity for air to penetrate or circulate. It remains wet for long periods after rain, and plant roots can rot in these conditions.

Soils that are either very sandy or a very heavy clay will require the addition of organic matter to balance their texture, improve drainage and add nutrients. Incorporate large quantities of well-aged animal manure (poultry, horse, cow or sheep) or some homemade compost. Other worthwhile soil improvers are Canadian sphagnum peat moss and organic soil mixes made from waste including milorganite.

Soil Drainage

This limits the range of plants that can be cultivated, because some varieties, including many shrubs and herbs, simply won't tolerate poorly drained growing conditions. To determine soil drainage in your garden, dig a hole to a depth of 1 foot and fill it with water. Within an hour the water should have drained away through the soil; however, if drainage is inadequate this will not occur. The fastest solution to bad drainage is to create raised beds, above ground level, by working plenty of light organic matter to the soil that will allow moisture to drain away easily after rain or watering. Serious drainage problems may require underground solutions, such as plastic drainage pipes laid at an angle to carry the water away from garden beds.

The pH Level

This refers to the acid or alkaline balance of the soil. It is important because certain species have specific preferences and requirements—camellias and rhododendrons, for example—and this chemical balance must be established before planting. Nurseries and garden centers sell simple pH testing kits that allow the gardener to ascertain the pH levels in various parts of the garden. Where soils are too acidic they can be balanced by the addition of some lime or dolomite, while alkaline soils generally respond well to the addition of well-aged animal manure or compost.

Budget

Shopping for plants can be costly, especially when trying to establish a new garden. Smart gardeners will learn some simple propagation techniques to increase their plant supply, such as taking cuttings or layerings from the gardens of friends and neighbors. Nursery plants can be purchased gradually, beginning with the larger-growing trees and shrubs, then moving down to perennials, bulbs and annuals as your budget allows.

Gardens are generally developed over a period of years, with new plants being added seasonally.

Maintenance Time

Gardeners with time limitations should avoid sensitive or difficult-to-grow species that require tender nurturing if they are to survive. Plants such as ferns can wither in a day or two if the soil is allowed to dry out, and if you do not have an automatic watering system these species will need constant monitoring and care. It is important to be realistic about the time you have available and your commitment to maintenance, to prevent losing valuable plants through unavoidable neglect.

AT THE NURSERY

When visiting a nursery, ask the advice of the owner or assistant, who should have some horticultural knowledge or qualifications. One of the advantages of shopping locally is that it is easy to get on-the-spot information and advice from someone who understands the problems associated with gardening in your particular area.

Select plants with a range of foliage colors and textures to add visual interest, but avoid jumbling too many different species together or the garden will lack harmony. Look for robust, healthy specimens. When plants have been well cared for in the nursery they will make the transition into your garden without a problem. However, if they have been neglected and under-watered they may have a ragged appearance and may even show some sign of disease. Plants that are pot-bound, or in potting mixture that appears depleted, should be avoided.

When you get your plants home, remember that they should be planted as quickly as possible. Leaving potted plants hanging around for weeks will result in a deterioration of their condition. If storing plants for any length of time, ensure they are kept in a sheltered, shaded situation, and do not allow the potting soil to dry out.

*RIGHT: The bright magenta flowers of the Armeria cranesbill (*Geranium psilostemon *syn.* G. armenum) *are made even more dramatic because of their black eyes and purple-bronze foliage. As a perfect foil, lamb's ears (*Stachys byzantina) *with clumps of felted silver leaves create a contrast, backed by slender, colorful spikes of lupines (*Lupinus sp.*).*

PLANT ASSOCIATIONS

Plants for All Soils

It is just as important to group plants together according to their physical requirements as it is to group them for their visual appeal. In certain situations the climate, soil or topography can place limitations on gardeners by pre-determining what species will survive. Once you understand the specific requirements of each plant, planning is much easier.

ACID-LOVING PLANTS

A good example of these plant associations is the combination of azaleas and rhododendrons, both delightful forest understorey plant types that prefer good light but protection from strong, direct sun and drying winds. An acid (lime-free) soil that is well drained and rich in

LEFT: Rich in color and texture, a flower border that includes pink dahlias, yellow and orange rudbeckias, stonecrop (sedum), gay feather (liatrus) and windflowers (anemone). This style of border is characterized by plants being grouped together in distinct clumps according to size, shape and flower color, rather than the more haphazard overlapping effect, seen in less formal settings.

PREVIOUS PAGE: A pleasing combination for either a sunny or semi-shaded position: slender spikes of warm yellow lupines (lupinus), white and pink foxgloves (digitalis) and pretty blue bellflowers (campanula). Here controlling slugs and snails will be important, especially when the plants are young and vulnerable to attack.

ABOVE: Camellias thrive in acid soil that is well-drained and rich in humus. Mulch the soil surface to suppress weed growth and prevent the soil surface drying out.

organic matter is essential if they are to remain healthy and produce a magnificent flower display. Not only must these conditions be provided, but surrounding plants should also have similar requirements. Create, in a climate that is cool enough, a scene with a mixture of azaleas and rhododendrons and a range of other plants, including a magnificent spring-flowering magnolia; some pretty camellias, both *Camellia reticulata* and *C. sasanqua*, and fragrant daphne or gordonia as a background plante

Other species that thrive in acid soils include all erica (heather); the shimmer-ing *Larix leptolepis* (Japanese larch); *Liquidambar styraciflua* with its brilliant orange-red autumn foliage; the conifers *Chamaecyparis obtusa* and *Cryptomeria japonica*; *Kalmia latifolia* (mountain laurel) with its tiny pale pink flowers; *Cornus kousa chinensis* (dogwood), durable hydrangeas; *Skimmia japonica*; *Pieris japonica*; *Acer palmatum* (maple); and *Berberis thunbergii*.

In a mixed bed or perennial border some of the best-loved varieties also prefer a slightly acid soil, and these include the more sensitive iris such as *I. ensata*; *Lilium tigrinum splendens* (a form of tiger

ABOVE: A clever way of creating a 'mixed bed effect' containing plants with the same basic requirements for soil and sunlight is to mass plant one species such as primula, seen here in a range of cultivars and varieties that differ dramatically in flower color and form. Foxgloves (Digitalis sp.) make a pretty backdrop.

lily) and *Lilium pardalinum* (panther lily); hybrid begonias; *Trillium erectum* and *Trillium grandiflorum*; lupinus hybrids (Russell lupines with their tall, colorful flower spikes); pretty primulas; *Narcissus cyclamineus* (a form of daffodil); *Gentiana sino-ornata,* a species of gentian; *Soldanella montana,* with its mauve fringed flowers; *Meconopsis betonicifolia* (Himalayan blue poppy); and *Shortia uniflora.*

In my own garden the soil's acid pH level was obvious when we bought the house, because one area of the garden featured a grouping of three major trees—sweet gum, maple and magnolia, underplanted with rhododendrons and barberry. I have subsequently added seven or eight large-growing azaleas and a thicket of hydrangeas, as well as naturalizing jonquils in the lawn. An added factor of great benefit is the delightful overhanging *Pinus patula* (Mexican pine) from my neighbor's garden which sheds a year-long supply of pine needles to mulch the soil surface and maintain the acid balance. *Pinus radiata* (Monterey pine) is well known for this purpose, and is often seen as a background plant to acid-loving species. For azaleas and camellias, in particular, this mulch layer is very important, as they are shallow-rooted and resent having the soil surface dry out. Nothing is better for keeping the soil moist than a thick layer of mulch, and nothing is better for these particular plants than a mulch of acid pine needles!

In other areas of the garden I have altered the pH for the cultivation of a wider range of plants, although I seem to need to keep adding lime or dolomite in these areas as the soil wants to revert to its natural state. So it seems that having an acid soil is not necessarily a limiting factor in creating a beautiful garden.

ALKALINE-LOVING PLANTS

Another common situation is soil that is alkaline, and not suited to growing all the beautiful plants described above. While there are plenty of good plants for alkaline soil, it is a shame to miss out on growing azaleas or camellias just because the pH is not quite right, so if the soil is alkaline some remedial action may be taken. Other factors, of course, such as good drainage and moisture retention are involved. However, I have found that adding lots of well-aged organic matter to the ground—animal manures and compost are excellent—and mulching with pine needles and pine bark make a great difference.

When you are thinking of plants that prefer a slightly alkaline soil pH, the choice is once again wide and varied. Among my favorites are all the varieties of prunus (flowering cherries), such as *P.* 'Amanogawa' and *P.* 'Tai-Haku', with their spring blossoms that attract bees to the garden. The slow-growing *Cercis siliquastrum* (Judas tree), with its rose-purple blooms, and all the hibiscus species (rose mallow), are also suited to these growing conditions. *Buddleia davidii* (butterfly bush) is a hardy, easy-to-grow large shrub that thrives in alkaline conditions, as do most of the hebe genus, although they are a little more sensitive and must have a sunny location.

Perennials for alkaline soils include hybrid bearded iris; the tall spikes of

ABOVE: *Group together plants according to their particular soil requirements as well as according to their preference for sun or shade. This mixed perennial border includes yarrow (*Achillea sp.*), catnip (*Nepeta sp.*), shasta daisies (*Chrysanthemum x superbum*), and lady's mantle (*alchemilla*) all of which have a similar preference for moderately rich, well-drained soil that still retains moisture well.*

kniphofia; glorious *Papaver orientale* (oriental poppy), with its huge, delicate flowerheads; *Linaria purpurea* (toadflax); *Echinops ritro*; verbascum (mullein); the salvias; camomile; the yarrows; scabiosa; brilliantly colorful coreopsis; *Linaria purpurea* (toadflax); and sedum (stonecrop). Fragrant thymus (thyme) in all its forms can be grown here too, along with lavendula (lavender) and dianthus.

So, when planning a colorful bed or border combine some of the above species with annuals such as *Anthirrhinum majus* (snapdragon); *Gypsophila elegans*; *Chrysanthemum carinatum*; scabiosa (pincushion flower); the 'Excelsior hybrids' of *Linaria maroccana*; *Cheiranthus cheiri* (wallflowers); and *Centaurea cyanus* (vivid blue cornflowers). Interestingly, members of the tulipa genus (tulips) prefer an alkaline soil, and can be grown if the climate is cool and the drainage is adequate. In warm regions tulip bulbs will need to be lifted and stored each season, then replanted in autumn.

PLANTS FOR CLAY SOILS

Soil that is heavy and clayey in consistency will make growing conditions difficult for some species, yet there are still quite a few worthwhile plants that can adapt to this situation. Daffodils (narcissus) are one of the few suitable types of bulbs. Although they naturally prefer better drainage, they will still give quite good results in heavy soil.

Perennials include *Polemonium caeruleum* (Jacob's ladder), with its decorative feathery foliage; *Lythrum virgatum*, which has spikes of rose-pink flowers mid-summer; *Monarda didyma* (bee

balm), a clump-forming perennial with rose-pink summer flowers; hemerocallis (day lily), with its showy summer flowers; *Digitalis grandiflora* (foxglove) with its willowy spikes of bell-flowers; *Doronicum plantagineum* (leopard's bane), which has bright yellow flowers from mid-spring; all the pretty asters (Michaelmas daisies), including *A. novae-angliae* and *A. novi-belgii*; *Inula hookeri*, which has showy yellow flowers from summer to autumn; the bright yellow rudbeckia (black-eyed Susan); and solidago (golden rod). Japanese anemones (*Anemone x hybrida*), too, will grow in heavy soils, growing strongly after two or more seasons.

Worthwhile shrubs for clay soils include *Forsythia suspensa*; spiraea 'Anthony Waterer'; *Salix hastata*; *Chaenomeles speciosa*; and cotoneaster.

PLANTS FOR WET SOILS

Waterside plantings can be beautiful, especially beside a shimmering pond, pool or stream. Landscaping around a watergarden is quite an art, and some knowledge of suitable species is important. Some gardens, too, have areas of boggy ground, and these can be used to create a delightful 'bog' garden, although the terms 'delightful' and 'bog' may seem contradictory.

Iris laevigata has softly colored foliage and subtle blue flowers in summer, and can be planted at the water's edge. The feathery pink flowers of *Filipendula rubra venusta* (meadowsweet) can be contrasted with *Iris sibirica* 'Perry's Blue', which has rich blue flowers; both flower in summer. Some lobelias and hostas can be grown in

damp soils, as can the ligularias, which have attractive heart-shaped leaves. *Lysichiton,* a genus of hardy perennials with amazing lily-like flowers, needs wet and fertile conditions, while *Orontium aquaticum* (golden club) can be grown at the margins of ponds, and features unusual spiky yellow flowers against mid-green foliage. For color consider trollius (globe flowers) in white, yellow or ivory; *Lythrum salicaria* (purple loosestrife); bog irises, *Caltha palustris* (marsh marigolds); various primulas; and hemerocallis (day lily). Bog arum will form a pretty edge to a small pool, while *Rodgersia pinnata* 'Superba' is a bog plant with excellent foliage and soft pink flowers mid-summer. Astilbes love moist soil, and the hybrids *Astilbe x arendsii* make a beautiful display planted in full sun or partial shade.

PLANTS FOR
DRY, SANDY SOILS

Soil that has a high sand content loses moisture quickly, and demands the addition of manures and other organic matter to improve its water-retention qualities. In many ways this soil is easier to remedy than heavy clay, although it may need constant mulching to build its friability and fertility. Many plants prefer a light, airy soil and so it is not hard to group together species that prefer this particular growing environment.

The glorious tall, creamy-white flower stalks of *Yucca gloriosa* and the brilliant yellow flowers of *Spartium junceum* are examples of plants that can be grown in dry, sandy soils. *Yucca filamentosa*, too, is

ABOVE: A waterside planting of lady's mantle (alchemilla), Siberian flag iris (Iris sibirica), and mimulus in soil that is rich and moist, yet not completely waterlogged. Ponds edged in plants that overhang the edges have a much more natural appearance, and often this style of planting is essential to cover pool lining or edging materials.

suitable, along with the cytisus group of brooms. The achillea (yarrows) can cope with hot and dry conditions, as can *Erysimum hieraciifolium* (Siberian wallflower), and *Dimorphotheca barberae* (Cape marigold) with its pretty clear pink flowers. California poppies (*Eschscholzia californica*) are colorful and hardy enough to withstand quite harsh summer weather, while *Tropaeolum majus* (nastur-

tiums), *Helipterum manglesii* (everlastings) and *Calamintha nepetoides* will help bring color to a flower bed or border. The perennials sedum (stonecrop) and gaillardia (blanket flower) are useful, while the annual *Portulaca grandiflora* seems to thrive in sunny, open situations or as part of a rockery. The seeds of pretty carpeting *Lobularia maritimum* (sweet alyssum) can be scattered

between other annuals and perennials, while the brilliantly colored blooms of *Mesembryanthemum criniflorum* can only be enjoyed in full sun, as they fold their petals when the sun recedes. *Armeria caespitosa* (thrift), *Dianthus alpinus* (pinks), *Iberis sempervirens* (candytuft) and *Gypsophila repens* will do well in exposed beds or sloping sites where water drains away freely.

ABOVE: Azaleas are members of the rhododendron genus, a large group of acid-loving plants that are prized for their prolific flowers in a wide range of colors from pure white through pinks, creams, apricots, oranges, purples and blues to deepest red. When planted in full sun, azalea flowers have a tendency to collapse during the hottest part of the day — dappled sunlight gives better results.

SHADE-LOVING PLANTS

Every garden has areas of shade, caused by overhanging eaves, mature trees or shrubs, a fence, a wall or even the house itself. These dark corners can be problematic, especially if conditions are also dry and the soil is depleted. Obviously, the ground at the base of established trees and shrubs tends to be inadequate for growing most plants, because the plant roots have taken so much moisture and nutrient. Even when there is a copious amount of leaf litter and mulch, these areas often need additional soil builders to make the areas suitable for planting anything at all. I have found that a good solution is creating built-up beds using rock to form dry stone walls or logs to create low-maintenance edgings. Behind the edges I pile mounds of homemade compost and well-aged manures, to create a healthy growing environment for shade-loving species. I make sure that when I water the beds are given a thorough soaking, as there is a risk of the tree roots traveling upwards in search of moisture if the beds have only been given a shallow watering.

What can you plant in this situation? Obviously, the choice is somewhat limited, especially if the shade is deep. In 'The shady garden' in Chapter 5, I have listed plants suited to dry and deep shade. For dappled shade, rhododendrons, azaleas and camellias are ideal, along with daphne, foxgloves, hostas and hydrangeas. Bulbs like freesias, daffodils and jonquil can also be grown in semi-shade if good soil is provided.

POLLUTION-RESISTANT PLANTS

Air pollution is damaging to the natural environment as well as to the human population, and city gardens that are constantly exposed to fumes, grime and other irritants suffer many problems. Robust plants are necessary to withstand these harsh growing conditions, and city gardeners must be on the lookout for suitable species when planning and planting.

Trees such as *Morus alba* and *Morus nigra* (mulberry trees), *Tilia x europaea* (common linden), *Catalpa bignonioides* (Indian bean tree) and *Robinia pseudoacacia* (black locust) are all known for their durability in this situation. Spring blossoms can still be enjoyed, as the *Prunus* species (flowering cherries and plums) is tolerant of pollution, while the golden-yellow spring flowers of the laburnum will also survive quite difficult conditions. In general, plants with tough, leathery foliage seem to stand a better chance of coping with grime and dirt, which is why hebe, genista (broom), olerearia (daisy bush) and *Weigela florida* are useful. The pretty flowers of the lilac (*Syringa vulgaris*) and the mock orange (philadelphus) will brighten up a courtyard garden in spring and summer. Roses, believe it or not, are very tough plants, and ideal for city gardens, while the magnolia is also quite suitable. In cooler regions rhododendrons and camellias should be planted. For spring and summer berries choose crataegus and *Pyracantha coccinea* (firethorn).

ABOVE: Rhododendrons are best grown in cooler climates, with rich moist soil and plenty of organic mulch to protect the shallow root system. Once established they are hardy and reliable, producing masses of dramatic flowers from late winter to mid-summer, according to the variety.

STYLE OPTIONS

White on White in Spring

White, in its various hues, is a dramatic tool for landscaping, as an accent or background plant; it is dramatic for a massed planting, or as part of a mixed bed or perennial border. The fresh brightness of white stands out, almost glowing, and at certain times of the day, such as dusk, it takes on a luminous quality. White plants are most effective when positioned in a bed that can be viewed easily at dusk.

In our small walled courtyard garden two forms of white tulip—tulipa 'White Emperor' (syn. 'Purissima') and 'Mount Tecoma'—have been grouped together in a small massed planting surrounding a

LEFT: A simple blue and white color scheme in which the whites are predominant. White is one of the most useful colors in the garden, drawing the eye and glowing strongly, especially in the late afternoon or early evening light. Most white flowers are not pure white at all, but tinged with cream, blue, pink or lavender. The intensity of white can be affected by surrounding plants, which will sometimes reflect their colors onto the white flowers.

PREVIOUS PAGE: Roses can be integrated successfully into the mixed border, as seen here with Rosa centifolia *and rosa 'Cerise Bouquet' combined with foxgloves (*Digitalis sp.*),* Nicotiana alata *and* Nicotiana x sanderae. *The roses have been staked to prevent their pendulous flowering stems from collapsing onto the perennials that edge the bed, and space has been left at their base to allow free air circulation.*

stone ornamental statue. A sprinkling of vivid blue myosotis (forget-me-nots) at the base of the tulips seems to throw the starkness of their white petals into even stronger contrast with the mid-green foliage and the warm hues of the stonework. 'White Emperor' is an early spring-flowering single form of tulip, with tall slender stems, while 'Mount Tecoma' is a peony-flowered double variety with slightly shorter stems. Modern hybrid tulips are grouped in divisions according to their main characteristics and flowering times. They vary from the simple single form to quite showy doubles, and are generally treated as annuals by being lifted each season—they rarely perform well if left in the ground year after year. White tulips are quite unusual; the other valuable variety is 'Glacier', which begins as a delicate white bud opening to a cream flower.

However, there are plenty of other white spring-flowering bulbs that could be used effectively in a white-on-white theme garden: pure white and creamy-white crocus, *Leucojum vernum* (spring snowflake); *Puschkinia scilloides* 'Alba'; various creamy-white fragrant freesias; *Galanthus nivalis;* and many varieties of narcissus (daffodil, jonquil), including 'Vigil', 'Chinese White', 'Paper White Grandiflora' and 'Thalia'.

When planning a white theme garden, be aware that there are many hues and tints of white, which can be warm (the

creams) or cool (those tinged with blue). Take, for example, the stark white of the Japanese anemone or the delicate snow-white tiny flowers of *Omphalodes linifolia* (Venus navelwort), and compare them with the chalky white blooms of *Iberis sempervirens* or the creamy color of 'White Swan' freesias or fragrant gardenias. These whites actually complement each other when grouped together, with added effect if placed against a contrasting backdrop of silver/gray foliage or deepest green.

In spring it is possible to plan a garden that includes white-flowering climbers as a background, then a combination of shrubs, perennials, bulbs, annuals and ground covers that flower in succession. White climbers include *Jasminum polyanthum*; *Clematis recta*; *Stephanotis floribunda*; and *Beaumontia grandiflora*. Shrubs for spring include white syringa (lilac); *Magnolia stellata*; *Choisya ternata;* and *Hebe canterburiensis*. In a cottage garden the tall flower spikes of the white form of digitalis (foxgloves) make an impressive display en masse, while sweet alyssum, *Iberis amara* and impatiens are worthwhile additions. Clumps of *Paeonia emodi* are a perfect spring-flowering perennial for such a design, contrasting with the white flower spikes of *Smilacina racemosa*.

Don't overlook the beauty of white roses—old garden roses such as 'Boule de Neige', *Rosa x. dupontii* and the damask 'Madame Hardy', or the glowing white of the floribunda 'Iceberg'.

White on White in Spring

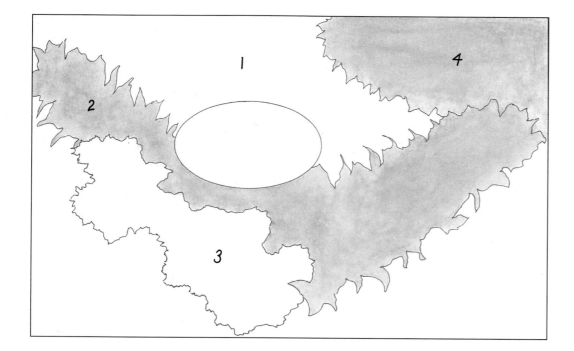

Key to planting plan

1. White tulips H. 6–8 inches
2. White tulips ('Mount Tecoma')
H. 8 inches
3. Forget-me-nots (*Myosotis alpestris*)
H. 4–6 inches
4. White climbing clematis (*Clematis recta*)
H. 10 feet

A small white on white flower bed will glow luminously at dusk. A massed clump of tulips includes two distinct varieties — each with a totally different flower shape. The bed is edged with bright blue forget-me-nots (*Myosotis alpestris*), while the stone wall in the background is covered with the white climber *Clematis recta*. After flowering, the tulip foliage must be allowed to die back completely; in warm climates the bulbs may be lifted and stored in a cool, dark place for replanting in autumn.

The Pastel Spring Border

Simplicity is of the essence when arranging plants to complement each other. In pastel groupings this is of particular importance, as varieties with subtle colors can easily be overwhelmed by blooms of a more intense hue. There are plenty of spring-flowering plants in pale shades—pinks, lilacs, soft yellows and creams—that make wonderful combinations.

These 'China Pink' tulips, which have been overplanted with viola 'Joker' in a narrow bed edging a rustic dry stone wall, are soft and subtle, yet make tremendous impact. The delicacy of the pastel blooms is accentuated by the weathered surface of the wall, and framed by the rich green of the lawn. The same effect could be achieved by planting a pastel border in front of a deep-green conifer or box hedge, which would throw forward the petal colors beautifully.

Alternatively, a background plant with silver/gray foliage, such as artemesia (wormwood), the felted leaves of verbascum (mullein), senecio cineraria or *Stachys byzantina* (lamb's ears), would be a charming combination. It is one that was favored by Gertrude Jekyll, who believed that combining silver foliage and pastel flowers made the pastel tints seem stronger.

To help you with decisions about color, look at the simple rules of art and nature. This will develop an eye for pleasing combinations. Just absorbing and appreciating the colors used by the Impressionist artists will give you a valuable guide to how petal and foliage shades can be used in the garden. Light is an important element too, as it greatly alters the intensity of color in various situations. Beds that are flooded with early morning light project colors quite differently from those exposed to the harsh midday sun of summer. Flowers grown in dappled shade may appear richer in color that those in bright sunlight; this is very obvious in the way various species perform in different countries and climates. The brightness of the light therefore becomes a consideration when planning which colors to combine in any garden scene. Pale shades may well be completely leeched of color if the light is too harsh!

With pastels it is possible to design a theme garden—say, one of pale pink or pale lavender—or to combine the various pastels in a mixed bed or border. Some pale pinks for spring include paeonia 'Sarah Bernhardt'; *Primula sinensis* and *malacoides*; various pale pink tulips; *Chionodoxa forbesii*; many of the low-growing cyclamens; and annuals, including *Bellis perennis* (English daisy) and matthiola (stocks). Later in the season, it is possible to consider one of the pale pink astilbes or *Malva moschata*, which has arching branches of mid-green foliage and a profusion of pale pink, saucer-shaped blooms. In the lavender or pale lilac color spectrum, consider several of the campanula varieties, lobelia, the feathery flowers of ageratum, *Nigella damascena*, various phlox and the beautiful pale 'Blue Star' *Aquilegia caerulea* (columbine).

Cream is a useful pastel shade that is often overlooked, and yet contributes greatly to more subtle garden plans. Indeed, many plants classified as white are in fact cream, and these blooms are wonderful in combination with other pastel shades, especially yellows and pinks. In late winter or early spring the rich cream, nodding flowerheads of *Helleborus corsicus* make even the shady areas of the garden appear warm and inviting. Many of the 'white' violas in fact have creamy petals, as do various kinds of narcissus (daffodils and jonquils).

LEFT: The soft, pastel palette is favored by many, especially those who prefer an old-fashioned, romantic-style garden. White, pink, pastel blue, lavender, soft apricot and pale yellow flowers can be used most effectively in this type of design, either in massed plantings of one color, or in successive drifts. With pastels there is less chance of clashing colors, or of one color 'stealing the scene' by overwhelming the others.

The Pastel Spring Border

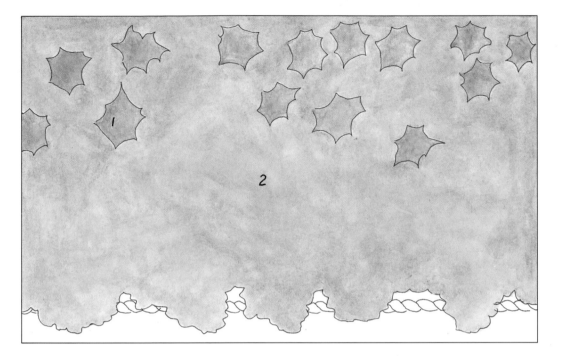

Key to planting plan

1. Pink tulips
2. Lavender pansies

A simple border, pale pink and pale lavender have been used together most effectively. Soft pink tulips are overplanted with a mass of lavender pansies, which will effectively hide the tulip foliage as it dies down after flowering. In a pastel garden design soft yellows and blues also look marvelous together, while cream and apricot are another romantic combination.

The Summer Cottage Border

The garden is a joy in summer, filled with warmth, color and the sounds of humming bees. A mixed border can really come alive at this time of the year, looking vibrant with its rich color schemes that reflect the mood of the gardener.

In our mixed bed of annuals, perennials and shrubs the overriding color themes are contrasting yellows and purples, highlighted by white or creamy-white accent plants. Tall spikes of delphinium 'Pacific Giants' frame the background edges, while solid evergreen foliage provides a background and a sense of perspective. A traditional English-style garden bench is almost enveloped by alchemilla (lady's mantle), with feathery lemon-yellow flowers and pale green foliage cascading onto the paved area. A combination of yellow daisies, *Achillea filipendulina* (yarrow), campanula and

LEFT: The garden in summer should be ablaze with color. In this garden mostly yellows, blues and lavender-pinks have been used harmoniously, with great care given to the height and mature spread of each species. At the side and back of the border, plants with tall flower spikes are accentuated by the deep green of the distant hedge, while the plants in the middle of the bed have been selected for their foliage texture as well as flower color. In the foreground plants have been chosen to cascade onto the paved area.

lilium 'Imperial Gold' fleshes out the center of the garden, providing flowers for long periods of the summer.

The value of the mixed border is both its versatility and the amazing array of flower combinations that can be achieved. A cottage-garden effect is easy to create, and is one situation where a wide range of contrasting colors can be used together happily—reds and yellows, oranges and blues, pinks and purples. The possibilities and permutations are countless, giving scope for every gardener to experiment and try new effects each season. Traditionally, a border was made up of clump-forming perennials, which generally flowered from summer through to autumn. However, the vogue now is to mix all kinds of plants into a flower border, including shrubs and roses, bulbs, annuals and ground covers. Annuals, in particular, are useful fast-flowering fillers, taking up space created by bulbs or perennials that have died back.

One of the hallmarks of the cottage-style border is the use of plants that form tall flower spikes, grouped around the edges and back of the garden. Old favorites such as digitalis (foxgloves), lupinus (lupines), alcae (hollyhocks), delphinium and consolida (larkspur) are probably the best known and best loved. Most will require some support in the

form of a slender stake as they grow, to prevent the flower spikes from being dashed by the wind. Plants with feathery flowers such as astilbes, gypsophila and Queen Anne's lace are also useful additions to the design, adding height and texture to the garden. For strong color accents, consider *Papaver orientale* (oriental poppies) with their huge papery petals, or brilliant Flanders poppies, which can be interplanted with *Centaurea cyanus* (cornflowers) for a dramatic red-and-blue color contrast.

To reduce seasonal planting, look for species that will self-sow and keep popping up year after year. Myosotis (forget-me-not) is a wonderful annual and a filler between other plants. However, it can become rather a nuisance as it may take over the garden unless kept in check. *Aquilegia vulgaris* (columbine) is a cottage-garden annual that readily reseeds, while *Lobularia maritima* (alyssum), *Lunaria annua* (honesty) and little violas (heart's-ease) are also valued for this quality. Others can be allowed to go to seed, and then the seed pods can be collected and dried for sowing the following autumn. Most hybridized annuals and biennials do not set seed, however, the old-fashioned varieties are perfect for this form of propagation.

The Summer Cottage Border

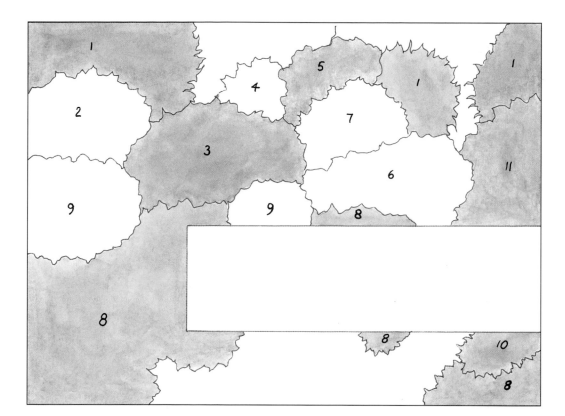

Key to planting plan

1. Delphiniums (delphinium 'Pacific Giants')
H. 4-5 feet
2. Lupines (lupinus 'Russell Hybrids')
H. 3 feet
3. Blanket flower (*Gaillardia aristata*)
H. 2 feet
4. Hollyhocks *(Alcea rosea)* H. 2 feet
5. Bellflowers (*Campanula gigante*)
H. 3.4 feet
6. Bellflowers (*Campanula persicifolia*)
H. 3.2 feet
7. Yarrow *(Achillea filipendulina)*
H. 3.4 feet
8. Lady's mantle (alchemilla)
H. 16 inches
9. *Stokesia laevis* H. 1 foot
10. Lilies (lilium 'Imperial Gold')
H. 6.5 feet

A successful border should overflow with plant varieties that have similar requirements, yet complement each other visually. This traditional flower bed contains delphiniums (delphinium 'Pacific Giants'), lupines (*Lupinus sp.*), *Gaillardia aristata,* hollyhocks (*Alcea rosea*), various species of bellflowers (*Campanula persicifolia* and *Campanula gigante*), wonderful yarrow (*Achillea filipendulina*), softly cascading lady's mantle (alchemilla), *Stokesia laevis* and tall spikes of lilies (lilium 'Imperial Gold'). This style of garden needs plenty of sun and frequent watering in summer.

The Green Summer Garden

In the heat of mid-summer nothing is more cooling than a green on green garden, where foliage plants are mingled to create a restful scene. Plants that are valued for their foliage often have more lasting appeal, as their attraction is not just dependent on a flashy show of flowers for a few weeks. Frequently green on green gardens are ideal for the shade or semi-shade, as they can produce lush results without the full blare of the summer sun.

In gardens where rich, moist soil is available, and there is no shortage of summer water, ferns are an ideal choice. While many ferns dislike very cold winters, there are plenty of species that are half-hardy and withstand quite severe winter temperatures. Maidenhair fern (*Adiantum sp.*) is a classic example, with its delicate stems and fronds. There are many other species suited to outdoor cultivation including the rough maidenhair (*Adiantum hispidulum*) which spreads to form a dense mass of foliage, growing to 16 inches in the right conditions. Another durable fern is the sword fern (*Nephrolepis exaltata*), which has erect or spreading lance-shape stems or fronds, growing to 3 feet. Another large grower is the soft shield fern (*Polystichum setiferum*) which will form a large clump of foliage if planted in a cool, damp and shaded place.

In warmer climates bromeliads can be a versatile choice for a green on green theme, with foliage in an amazing array of forms and showy flowers. In cooler regions they can be grown in containers, and taken indoors or into a greenhouse in winter. Most species are small enough for container cultivation.

Warm growing conditions are also required for the dieffenbachias, which have outstanding variegated foliage in rich greens and creams. *Alocasia cuprea* is an evergreen, tufted perennial with glossy green and purple leaves. It makes an impressive display when mass planted at the front of a bed or border. Like many plants with large leaves it dislikes winter frosts, and protection must be provided.

Hostas are also a natural choice, with lush clumps of foliage from late spring to late autumn. At the back of the border clumps of kniphofia 'Percy's Pride' will be most effective, with reed-like foliage and tall stems of cream flowers tinged with green. In cold areas the crowns need to be protected with a thick mulch in winter.

LEFT: Refreshing greens with a touch of cream are cooling in summer; a pleasant change from bright primary color schemes or pastels. Foliage plants and ferns can be the basis of a green on green border, with varied texture, leaf shape and height providing the essential visual contrast.

The Green Summer Garden

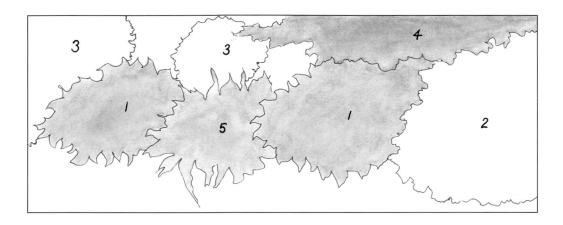

Key to planting plan

1. Hosta (*Hosta fortunei*) H. 3 feet
2. Lady's mantle (alchemilla) H. 16 inches
3. Valerian (*Valeriana officinalis*) H. 3 feet
4. Cream rose (*Rosa* 'Peace') H. 6 feet
5. Sword fern (*Nephrolepis exalta*) H. 3 feet

Although hostas thrive in full shade, they will do equally well in a
semi-shaded border, providing the soil is fertile and moist. Ferns have similar requirements,
making the two ideal companions in this situation. At the edge of the bed, lady's mantle
(alchemilla) has greenish-yellow flowers, but more notably rounded leaves with
crinkled edges that catch and hold water droplets after rain. This foliage contrasts well
with the deep green fronds of the sword fern (*Nephrolepis exalta*) and the large showy
foliage of the hostas.

The Blue Summer Garden

The blue color spectrum ranges from the cool, clear blues of *Meconopsis betonicifolia* (blue poppy) to the warm lilac-blues of *Nepeta cataria* (catnip). In a blue garden plan all shades and hues of blue can be combined effectively either in drifts or blocks of color. Although they tend towards the purple end of the spectrum, irises make an excellent display at the back of the border. Iris 'Harmony' and *Iris histriodes* 'Major' have strong blue flowers. *Iris* 'Memorial Tribute' has wonderful pale blue blooms, while *Iris laevigata* also has blue varieties, and makes an excellent plant in wet soil beside a pond or stream.

Also pale blue is the charming *Campanula persicifolia*, which grows to 3 feet with tall nodding spikes of cup-shaped light blue flowers. Some varieties of columbines (*Aquilegia vulgaris*) are also blue-purple, and these will self seed

LEFT: Blue and purple flowers are always fashionable, either blended together on their own, or mixed with white in a theme garden. The blues of delphiniums and cranesbills (Geranium sp.) tend to the purple end of the spectrum, richly contrasting with their mid-green foliage. Delphiniums give height to the middle and back of the border, while the geraniums cascade over the edge, softening the front of the garden.

easily in the garden, popping up season after season. For ease of cultivation the agapanthus is hard to beat, with fleshy clumps of foliage and dramatic circular blue flowerheads carried on top of tall, strong stems. Delphiniums are glorious in summer and into autumn, depending on the climate. Ideal for a cottage border, their slender flower spikes may require staking to prevent damage in windy weather.

Annuals are well represented in the blue color range, with ageratum and nigella being among the most useful. *Ageratum houstonianum* 'Blue Mink' is fast-growing, with clusters of feathery pale blue flowers from summer through into autumn. *Nigella damascena* 'Persian Jewels' has flowers of blue, pink and white which are often grown together, although seeds should be available in individual colors. Cornflowers (*Centaurea cyanus*) are among the best-loved blue annuals, and they make a wonderful display when mass planted in a sunny, open bed. At the front of the border *Lobelia erinus* or *Anchusa capensis* will make a marvelous blue edging, both growing to 8 inches and forming a carpet of foliage and blue flowers.

Yellow has traditionally been blended with blue in the garden and some plants

actually combine these colors within their flowers. Swan River daisy (*Brachycome iberidifolia*) is a spectacular annual with tiny fragrant bright blue flowers with yellow centers. The kingfisher daisy (*Felicia bergeriana*) has a similar color combination, also with pretty daisy-like flowers. The tiny blue flowers of the forget-me-not (*Myosotis sp.*) also have yellow centers, and are useful because they seed so easily throughout the garden. Indeed, without care, they will become invasive. Several varieties of pansies (*Viola sp.*) have clear blue blooms, including the pretty viola 'Azure Blue' which looks spectacular mass planted in a shallow terracotta pot.

In the rockery garden consider *Polygala calcarea* 'Bulley's Variety' which is an evergreen ground-covering plant with masses of deep blue flowers in late spring and summer. Fascinating fairy thimbles (*Campanula cochleariifolia*) send out runners as it spreads, with mid-green foliage and exquisite pale blue bell flowers over many weeks of summer. It is also a useful low-growing plant for a rockery or alpine garden.

Another vigorous creeping perennial is *Pratia pedunculata*, which has pale to mid-blue starry flowers, and makes a good ground cover in moist soil.

The Blue Summer Garden

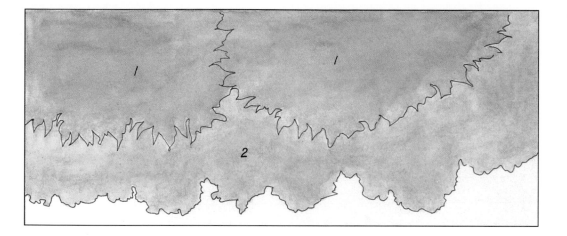

Key to planting plan

1. Delphiniums H. 4½ feet
2. Cranesbill (*Geranium sp.*) H. 2 feet

A pretty bright purple-blue border with a mixture of cranesbills (*Geranium sp.*) and delphiniums. Massed plantings always have great dramatic impact, accentuating the color and form of the plants used. Clumps of perennial cranesbills can be divided in autumn or spring to create new plants that will spread as they grow. Delphiniums, however, are usually grown as annuals, and seed will need to be planted in autumn or early spring to capture this massed effect.

The Romantic Summer Garden

Flower gardens are always popular, especially those with romantic, old-world charm. The gardens of Vita Sackville-West and Gertrude Jekyll are much admired, and both these gardeners are known for their preference for this particular style of landscaping.

The secret of a romantic garden is the way in which the plants are combined, softly overlapping and complementing each other both with flowers and foliage. Although certain flowers are sometimes mass-planted for color effect, there is more emphasis on a gentle combining of colors rather than bold statements.

Roses are an essential ingredient of the romantic garden. Heritage roses in particular, including all those wonderful old-fashioned ramblers and climbers, have a definite place; integrated into beds

and borders or allowed to clamber up into trees or cascade over walls, trellises or pergolas. Roses are marvelous in their adaptability, and even some of the larger growing ramblers can be tamed by regular pruning and kept to a manageable size even in quite a small garden. In a country garden, of course, they can be allowed to take off, their arching branches laden with blooms during summer. Look for varieties that are fragrant, and those with recurrent flowers for a prolonged display.

Perennials are synonymous with romantic-style gardens, especially those with tall flower spikes like foxgloves (*Digitalis sp.*), delphiniums, hollyhocks (*Alcea sp.*) and lupines (*Lupinus sp.*). If the garden has an area that is sunny and open, it will make an ideal border, which can be planted with perennials that are blended together thoughtfully. Position the taller growing species at the back of the bed, then gradually decrease the size of the plants towards the front, with low-growing species that will cascade onto the path along the edges. Shrub roses can be positioned throughout the bed, providing some space is left around their base to allow for free air circulation. A simple pergola can be constructed at the back of the bed for

climbing roses, creating a frame for the entire garden.

Plants with fragrant flowers or foliage are an important ingredient. Climbers such as jasmine (*Jasminium sp.*) and clematis will quickly cover a wooden trellis or pergola, framing a gateway or entrance. *Daphne odora* and lavender (*Lavandula sp.*) are both highly scented, and useful in beds or borders if good drainage is provided. *Magnolia stellata* is a wonderful deciduous tree with fragrant star-like white flowers that are flushed with pink. Lilacs (*Syringa sp.*) are also highly perfumed, and can be grown easily in a wide range of soils and conditions. Bulbs that are prized for their fragrance include freesias (*Freesia refracta*), day lilies (*Hemerocallis sp.*) and lily-of-the-valley (*Convallaria majalis*). Cottage pinks (*Dianthus sp.*) and violets (*Viola sp.*) are also worthwhile for their ease of cultivation as well as appealing fragrance.

No romantic garden would be complete without a trellis covered with sweet peas (*Lathyrus odoratus*) or a bed of wallflowers (*Cheiranthus cheiri*). These old-fashioned favorites are easy to grow and, although they are annuals that require replanting every season, are well worth the trouble.

LEFT: So many plants evoke the romantic garden atmosphere, including heritage roses and all those delightful species with aromatic flowers or foliage. In essence this garden should be quite feminine in appearance, with pastels or soft summer colors that are blended together with subtle style. Include some architectural features such as lattice or archways, and outdoor seating so that the garden can be enjoyed.

The Romantic Summer Garden

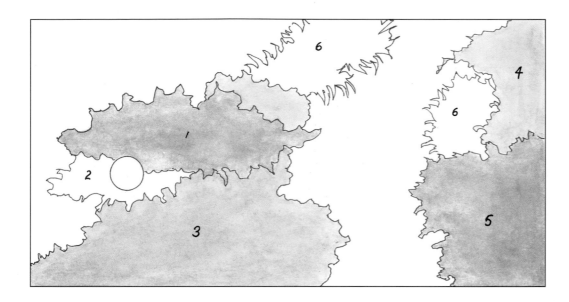

Key to planting plan

1. Pink climbing rose H. 13 feet
2. Clematis (large-flowering cultivar)
H. 6 feet
3. Cranesbill (*Geranium sp.*) H. 2 feet
4. Red rose (rosa 'Dortmund') H. 16 feet
5. Lady's mantle (alchemilla) H. 2 feet
6. *Lychnis viscaria* H. 1 foot

In the romantic garden include some climbing plants, such as clematis, and of course roses, that will fill the garden with fragrance over most of the summer. Here the clematis and climbing rose have been carefully intertwined on a single support; the clematis must have cool shade at root level to survive, while the rose needs sunlight and warmth to flower, so this is indeed a clever combination. Throughout the flowerbed old-fashioned favorites such as lady's mantle (alchemilla), cranesbill (*Geranium sp.*) and lychnis have been used effectively. In the background, a trellis creates privacy, and provides support for climbing roses.

The Hosta Walk in Autumn

The hosta or plantain lily is a prized foliage plant grown for its dramatic leaf colors and textures. There are many forms of hosta, including those with striking leaf markings in gold, white or cream. They are perennials, and as such are ideal for beds or borders, providing the growing conditions are cool, shady and moist.

In our setting a wide range of varieties have been grouped together to create a shady hosta walk, framing a path that leads through a cool woodland garden to a bench nestled in front of a lush shrub backdrop.

In a massed planting, hostas create a green-on-green theme garden, with foliage varying from a cool blue-green

LEFT: Cool and inviting, the lush green foliage of hostas forms a carpet framing a pathway that leads to a traditional garden seat. Hostas are popular perennials, valued for their glorious mounds of foliage, that are various shades of green and blue-green according to the variety. They are ideal for shady parts of the garden, although when planted beneath trees will require plenty of watering to keep the foliage healthy. Snail and slug protection is essential!

through every possible shade to warm yellow-greens, and those variegated with cream and gold. It is this range of luxuriant green foliage that gives a hosta walk visual interest, especially as the plants mature and overlap each other. Cultivars worth including in such a plan include *H. fortunei* 'Aurea Marginata', which has clear green leaves edged with cream; *H. undulata* var. *univittata,* which is bold green and white; *H.* 'August Moon', with its leaves of a strong clear green, and *H. tardiflora,* which features more slender, glossy foliage. Also look for *H. fortunei* 'Albopicta', *H.* 'Gold Standard', *H. sieboldiana* 'Frances Williams' and *H.* 'Halycon'.

Hostas vary in size from very small specimens that reach only 1 foot in height to clumps that can reach 5 feet in height and width after a few years' growth. The smaller-growing varieties are excellent for city courtyard gardens, while the larger forms can be incorporated in many situations in more spacious gardens. They are frequently used as waterside plants near pools and streams, as they require rich, moist soil to grow effectively. When creating a massed bed of hostas prepare the ground well prior to planting, adding plenty of well-aged manures, composts or

other organic matter. Hostas can either be grown from bare-rooted divisions in winter—often sold by mail order—or when in foliage, in spring or summer. They must be kept well watered during the warmer weather, and given protection from snails and slugs, which love to feast on their succulent foliage.

In a mixed bed, hostas look wonderful in combination with silver/gray foliage plants, and with species that have feathery flowers or foliage. This combination works well because the strong outline of the hostas provides a solid contrast to other, more fragile, foliage. Allow space for the young plants to grow and develop, because even if they are quite compact in the first year, they will quickly spread and will need space to create a more dramatic display.

Like most perennials, hostas die back in winter, disappearing beneath the soil surface. They should be mulched well with manure and leaf mulch, and the soil should not be allowed to dry out too much while the plants are dormant. In summer they will produce elegant flowerheads borne on tall spikes above the foliage. The flowers vary considerably according to the cultivar, and many are quite inconspicuous.

The Hosta Walk in Autumn

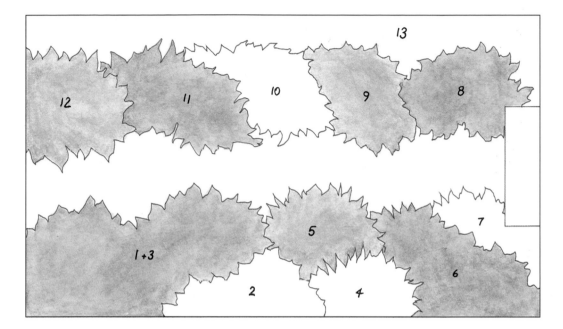

Key to planting plan

1. *Hosta sieboldiana* H. 4 feet
2. *Hosta sieboldiana* var. 'Elegans' H. 4 feet
3. *Hosta sieboldiana* H. 4 feet
4. *Hosta lancifolia* H. 20 inches
5. *Hosta crispula* H. 30 inches
6. *Hosta ventricosa* H. 27 inches
7. Hosta 'Gold Standard' H. 30 inches
8. Hosta 'Royal Standard' H. 2 feet
9. *Hosta sieboldiana* 'Frances Williams'
H. 4 feet
10. Hosta 'Halycon' H. 1 foot
11. *Hosta plantaginea* H. 2 feet
12. Hosta 'August Moon' H. 2 feet
13. Silver Birch (*Betula pendula*) H. 70 feet

Although the flowers are inconspicuous, the foliage of the hosta makes it a desirable addition to the shaded parts of your garden. When mass planted they look particularly effective, especially when a wide range of varieties are massed together, to highlight the differences of foliage color, size and texture. In this grouping foliage varies from green and white variegated to bright light green and muted blue-green.

The Blue/Purple Garden in Autumn

Autumn is synonymous with the glow of leaves; turning to new colors: oranges, reds and yellows, that flood the garden with light and warmth. However, there is a cool side to autumn too, not just in the gradual drop of temperature, but also in the flowering of plants in the blue/purple spectrum.

In our scene the majestic *Sorbus hupehensis* is underplanted with hydrangeas and agapanthus, two of the most robust and easy-to-grow plants in numerous situations. Indeed, agapanthus are virtually indestructible. They seem to thrive even in the most depleted conditions. It is hard to find plants that can grow in shade, especially dry shade. However, these two beauties will do so quite admirably. They will start to flower in summer, and remain splendid through early autumn, as the leaves begin to turn.

LEFT: Cool blues and purples look appealing in the shade, and help to ensure that autumn colors are not just limited to the familiar reds, yellows and oranges often seen during this season. Shaded areas of the garden require hardy species, that can withstand not just a lack of sunshine, but often quite dry conditions. Hydrangeas and agapanthus are ideally suited to this situation, both genus noted for their ability to thrive in poorer soils and areas that do not receive much rain.

As with all the color groups, blues vary tremendously across the spectrum, from the clear blue of forget-me-nots and bluebells to the many shades of lilac, mauve, violet and lavender. Warm and cool blues and purples can be combined effectively, and they can also be teamed with many other colors: a blue and white garden is always admired, while yellow and blue/purple is a classic combination. Red flowers seem even more red when positioned beside blue-flowering species, and the combination of blue and orange can be quite dramatic, if not a little overwhelming.

In late summer and early autumn *Tibouchina urvilleana* (lasiandra) will produce masses of deep violet/blue flowers. This large evergreen shrub, growing to 12 feet, makes a perfect screening plant, as the background to a flower bed or border. Smaller shrubs in the blue range include *Ceratostigma willmottianum,* which starts flowering in late summer and produces foliage that turns red in late autumn, and some of the fuchsias—those with blue/purple and mauve flowers. The evergreen twining climber *Billardiera longiflora* actually flowers in summer, but this is followed by a beautiful display of purple-blue berries in autumn.

There are a few worthwhile perennials for this time of the year, including *Aster novi-belgii* and *Aster x frikartii*, and the tall *Gentiana asclepiadea* (willow gentian), which has arching sprays of deep blue trumpet-shaped flowers. For the front of the bed *Aster amellus* is a pretty choice, covered with bright blue daisy flowers with yellow centers. *Liriope muscari* also blooms now, displaying spikes of rounded blue-purple flowers above glossy dark-green foliage. A useful ground cover or rockery plant with vivid blue flowers is *Gentiana septemfida;* also useful are the smaller-growing *G. x macaulayi* and *G. sino-ornata.* Annuals can be planted mid-summer to flower in autumn in more temperate climates: consider cornflowers, ageratum, *Nigella damascena* and *Convolvulus tricolor.*

Perhaps the most attractive surprise of autumn is the appearance of drifts of vivid fall-blooming crocus through the lawn. Several species of crocus have blue/purple flowers, and they bring a special magic to the garden, appearing just as the weather experiences its first bite of cold. One of my favorites is *Crocus speciosus* 'Oxonian', which has deep violet/blue flowers.

One omission in the blue flower brigade is the rose, although this is being remedied via genetic engineering. Over the years breeders have introduced some lilac/lavender shaded roses such as 'Blue Moon' and 'Blue Peter'. However, scientists are now developing a clear blue rose, using genetic material from a petunia.

The Blue/Purple Garden in Autumn

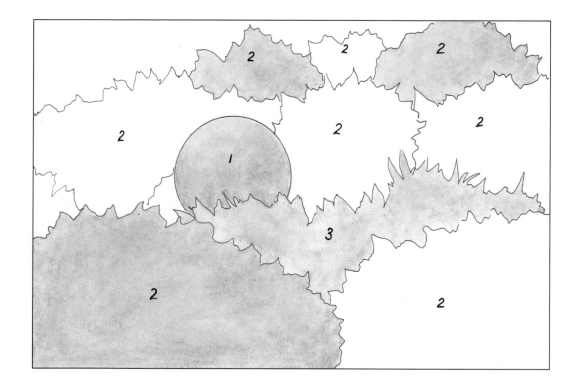

Key to planting plan

1. Mountain ash (*Sorbus hupehensis*) H. 40 feet
2. *Hydrangea macrophylla* H. 4–6 feet
3. African lily (*Agapanthus campanulata*)
H. 2–3 feet

Successful landscaping at the base of trees provides a challenge, as the growing conditions here are often depleted and dry, as well as shady. In this situation a mixture of hydrangeas and agapanthus provide an easy solution, due to their hardiness and ease of cultivation. This combination works well visually, as the foliage of the two species complement each other, while the flowers are contrasting in tone and texture. The soil should be neutral to alkaline for the best results.

The Winter Woodland Garden

Although the garden may appear to sleep in winter, there is always some activity, some small bud or flower or berry to maintain interest. As winter draws to an end certain bulbs begin to emerge, among the earliest of them the crocus, in pure shades of white, lilac, purple or violet. The effect of a massed planting of crocuses is spectacular, as in this woodland scene, where various colors have been combined and inter-planted with clumps of *Leucojum vernum* (spring snowflake) and *Galanthus nivalis* (snowdrop).

Crocuses are very surprising bulbs: the flowers and petals are quite large and showy, yet appear very soft and fragile; the stems are short, holding the blooms very close to the ground. Some varieties display the flowers before foliage, and in

LEFT: Although winter may be stark, it can hold some wonderful color surprises as certain species beat the odds and come into flower. In cold climates the emergence of late winter flowering bulbs is particularly exciting, especially if snowfall has been masking the soil surface for several months. Indeed many bulbs need these cold, crisp conditions to perform at their best, and will not produce good results in more temperate climates.

regions that experience heavy winter snow the crocuses thrust their colorful petals through the white carpet, creating a magical effect.

Bulbs naturalized beneath deciduous trees are the hallmark of a woodland garden. The effect is achieved by scattering the bulbs on the soil surface, then planting them where they fall. Over a period of years the bulbs multiply, and a carpeting effect is achieved.

In gardens where the soil at the base of established trees is depleted, it may be necessary to improve the growing conditions before planting the bulbs. This can be done by aerating the soil with a fork, then lightly incorporating some well-aged animal manure or compost. Water the ground well to help soften the entire area. Unless the soil is soft and friable, planting in the lawn or on rough ground can be a chore—backbreaking work and hard on your hands. If you are planting a large area, invest in a bulb-planter, a hand tool designed to lift a core of soil, making a space for the bulbs. Make sure to plant deeply enough—one year I planted jonquils, and they were promptly pushed from the ground by their emerging roots. This was because

the soil beneath the hole was too hard for the roots to penetrate. It wasn't much fun replanting them!

There are many bulbs that can be naturalized in a woodland setting. Some of the early flowering narcissus (daffodils, jonquils) appear in late winter. Among the daffodils, the trumpet and large-cupped varieties flower early in the season, with blooms of white, cream, pink and pure yellow, depending on the variety. Among my favorites are N. 'Trousseau', which has milk-white petals and a soft lemon trumpet; N. 'Oscar Ronald', with its creamy white petals and an apricot-pink cup that ages to a deeper pink, and N. 'Paper White Grandiflora', which has very fragrant, white star-shaped flowers—as many as 10 per stem. They seem to last for weeks, giving a magnificent display.

Lachenalias also flower in late winter, with spikes of fragrant bell-shaped flowers. In some areas *Erythronium dens-canis* (dog tooth violets) flower at the end of winter, although spring flowering is more usual. They look very pretty in a woodland garden, with mottled leaves and glorious pink, purple or white flowers banded with brown, purple or yellow near the center.

The Winter Woodland Garden

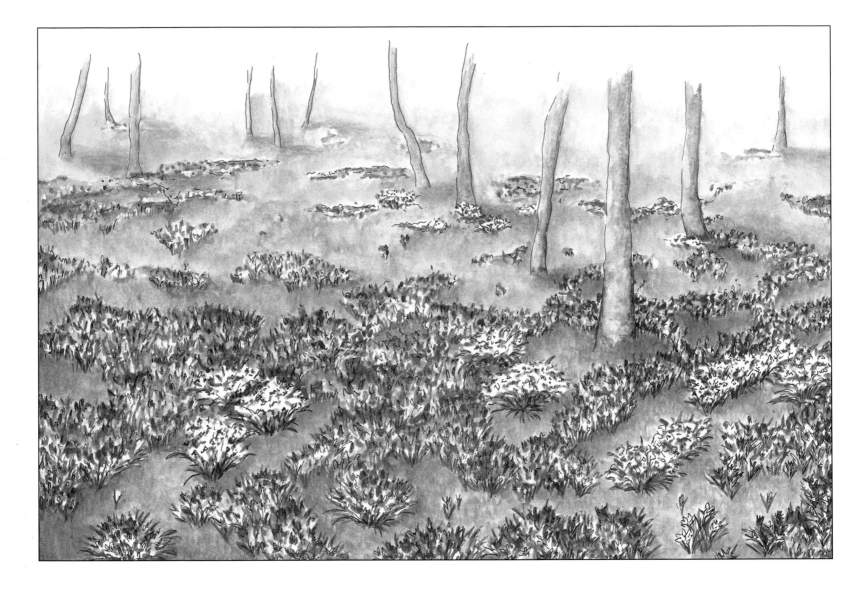

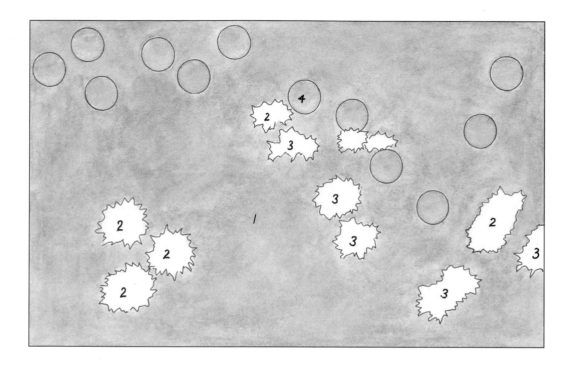

Key to planting plan

1. *Crocus* 'Snow Bunting', *C. tommasinianus*, *C. vernus* 'Princess Juliana'
H. 4 inches
2. Snowdrops *(Galanthus nivalis)*
H. 10 inches
3. Spring snowflake *(Leucojum vernum)*
H. 6 inches
4. Silver Birch *(Betula pendula)* H. 70 feet

A sea of color emerges as winter crocus and snowdrops come into flower in a massed planting through a copse of silver birch (*Betula pendula*). Care has been taken to naturalize the bulbs in drifts, avoiding the static feeling of rows or ordered beds. A mixture of crocus makes the scene more interesting — white *Crocus* 'Snow Bunting', lilac *Crocus tommasinianus* and mid-purple *Crocus vernus* 'Princess Juliana'. Both spring snowflakes (*Leucojum vernum*) and snowdrops (*Galanthus nivalis*) have been used, planted in rich clumps between the drifts

THE
GARDEN IN
SPRING

A Burst of New Life

At no other time of the year is the garden as exciting as it is in early spring. In all cultures spring is the time for renewal and regeneration, and in the garden it brings a flood of color and life, with a rapid explosion in the growth of foliage and flowers. Most gardeners experience a burst of energy; the landscape suddenly looks so fresh and pretty after months of virtual dormancy. And, just as the house is given a 'spring-clean', so it is also time to pour some of that energy into the garden. The warmer weather makes early-morning forays, even those before breakfast, a wonderful way of getting some gardening chores done. As the days lengthen the gardener can spend more hours planting and

LEFT: A startling color combination of warm pinks and blue; the deciduous mollis azalea rhododendron 'Irene Koster', which is covered in glorious flushed pink flowers with yellow eyes, and the hardy flowering stems of the bluebell (Hyacinthoides hispanica syn. Scilla campanulata) which multiply annually. Mollis azaleas prefer quite sunny, open conditions but have the same soil requirements as all rhododendrons.

PREVIOUS PAGE: Glorious tulips such as 'Attila' give their best display when mass planted, with strong stems topped by rich mauve-pink blooms. In many regions tulip bulbs must be lifted when the foliage has died back after flowering, and stored in a cool, dark place until time for replanting in autumn.

puttering, and admiring his or her handiwork.

Late spring- and summer-flowering annuals are usually sown from seed or planted as seedlings with the first warming of the soil. However, in areas that experience late spring frosts care must be taken, as tender young plants can easily be lost in a sudden blast of unexpected cold weather. The same applies for vegetable and herb seeds and seedlings planted at this time of the year. Some gardeners protect these tiny plants with glass or plastic until all danger of frost has passed. The other protection needed, of course, is from snails and slugs, which love to feast on tender young shoots. I prefer ducks, but snail pellets are probably more practical in most situations.

At the back of a flower bed or border, to create a cottagey effect, arrange clumps of *Alcea rosea* (hollyhocks), *Salvia sclarea* var. *turkestanica,* which is a fast-growing erect biennial, *Consolida ambigua* 'Imperial series' (larkspur) and *Campanula medium* (Canterbury bells). For something that will flower at the same time, consider a massed planting of *Nigella damascena* 'Miss Jekyll', which will give a glorious display of bright green feathery foliage and soft blue flowers. A scattering of yellow-flowered annuals such as *Coreopsis tinctoria* (tick-seed) or *Chrysanthemum segetum* will make a perfect foil for the blue flowers of nigella.

Spring is the time for bulbs, and with careful planning you should be enjoying a splendid display over many months, from late winter onwards. The earlier-flowering daffodils and jonquils will be followed by *Fritillaria imperialis* (crown imperial) with its showy orange bell-flowers, watsonias, *Dietes grandiflora* (wild iris) and *Cardiocrinum giganteum* (giant lily). Among the medium and smaller bulbs seen in spring are many members of the allium family; *Triteleia hyacinthina* (syn. *Brodiaea hyacinthina*); glorious ranunculus and anemones; pretty pink scilla, *Hyacinthoides hispanica* (syn. *Scilla campanulata* (Spanish bluebells); and, of course, those wonderful tulips.

While bulbs give a truly magnificent display, many gardeners are irritated at the gap they leave after flowering has finished. The foliage must be allowed to wither naturally—it must never be clipped back or mowed over, as the dying-back process provides the nutrients for the following year's flowering. The gap can be quickly patched with annual seedlings, or, better still, the bulbs could have been overplanted with annuals the preceding autumn, which will emerge through the center when they flower, and then disappear gradually back into the annual's foliage. Remember that the soil will need to be quite rich to sustain this intensive growth, so dig in some organic fertilizer at planting time.

Perennials in Spring

As the weather warms, perennials will start to reappear, first the foliage and eventually the flowers, depending on the variety. They may need a boost of nutrients during this vigorous growing and flowering period, so mulch them with compost and apply a side dressing of blood and bone to ensure steady, healthy growth.

The larger perennials tend not to flower until summer, but anticipate some display from the polygonatum species (Solomon's seal) and most of the paeonia species (peony) now. The peony is one of the most spectacular flowering perennials, producing huge flowers from clumps of fresh foliage. It can be quite sensitive

LEFT: Blue and white is a much-loved combination, easy to achieve in spring by combining bluebells (Hyacinthoides hispanica syn. Scilla campanulata), and white wake robin (Trillium grandiflorum) plus the crinkled bronze foliage of Rodgersia aesculifolia, which will be soon covered with plumes of fragrant pinkish-white flowers.

to exposed conditions, and may require some support as the flowers appear. There are varieties, such as *P. emodi*, which have much smaller, more delicate flowers, also in spring.

Smaller perennials for spring flowering include *Trillium grandiflorum* (wakerobin) which relies on a cool, woodland setting to produce its startling white, three-petalled flowers against a background of deep green foliage; the pretty *Actinotus helianthi* which is quite shortlived but gives a wonderful display of gray-green felt-like foliage and creamy white flowers; *Anemone sylvestris* (snowdrop windflower), which forms a carpet of foliage from which fragrant white flowers emerge on slender stems; some of the smaller dianthus, including *D. plumarius* 'Pretty Ladies' and *D. plumarius* 'Earl of Essex'; and the soft pink *Osteospermum jucundum* (syn. *O. barberae*), which has a neat growth habit and masses of flowers if planted in moderately rich soil in full sun.

In temperate climates the *Smilacina racemosa* (False spikenard) will give a pretty display of feathery white flowers against a backdrop of light green foliage, followed by fleshy red fruits in early summer. The clump-forming *Ranunculus aconitifolius* grows to 2 feet and should be covered with pure white flowers and deep green foliage. It makes a pretty background plant to spring-flowering bulbs; and will continue to flower into summer.

For a splash of brilliant color a massed planting of *Tanacetum coccineum* 'Brenda' is hard to beat, with slender stems reaching 2 feet topped by daisy flowers of magenta with bright yellow centers. Choose a sunny position and water well if the weather gets warm. In the yellow color range is *Doronicum pardalianches* (Leopard's bane) noted for its pretty heart-shaped foliage and clear yellow daisy flowers which are borne above the foliage on slender spikes. It can be grown either in full sun or in partial shade, and will spread freely in an informal setting.

Trees

Flowering trees are at their peak during spring, and will provide much of the season's excitement. In the gardens of Japan spring blossom time is legendary, with massed plantings of ornamental cherries and plums (*Prunus* species) filling the landscape with the fragrance of their flowers. In the orchard many fruiting trees—apples, peaches, apricots and plums—give an equally delightful display. Of course, fruiting blossom trees can be just as successful when integrated into the ornamental garden, except that neglected fallen fruit may prove problematic in autumn. In any event, many of the 'ornamental' varieties seem to throw small fruits, which can be gathered and used for jams and syrups.

One of the earliest blossom trees to flower is *Prunus x blireiana*, a very fast-growing small tree with splendid purple foliage, aging to bronze, and a spectacular display of pink blossom flowers. It can be pruned to shape, or espaliered against a wall or fence. Flowering cherries and plums are often grown as street trees or in groves, to line a driveway or entrance. However, as a single-specimen tree, *Prunus persica* is hard to beat, with its short trunk, wonderful bark and vase-shaped limb formation. There are many varieties, including *P. persica* 'Double White' and 'Double Crimson', and the amazing *P. persica* 'Versicolor', which has pink and white striped flowers on the same branch as either plain white or plain pink flowers. Other blossom trees of note include *P. sargentii* (sargent cherry); *P. subhirtella* 'Pendula rubra', which has weeping branches of deep pink flowers; *P.* 'Hokusai'; and *P.* 'Accolade'.

Of all the spring-flowering trees the dogwood (cornus species) is my favorite. There are so many aspects of this species to admire—the elegant form, the colored stems in winter, the shapely foliage, glorious four-bracted 'flowers' and showy fruits. The best flowering dogwoods include *C. florida*, *C. kousa chinensis* and *C. nuttallii*, which should have well-drained acid soil and full sun to produce good results; *C. alba* (red-barked dogwood), which has deep green foliage and creamy-white flowers; *C. controversa* 'Variegata'; *C. canadensis;* and *C.* 'Sibirica'. *Cornus alternifolia* 'Argentea' is a handsome specimen with silver-green foliage and small cream flowers in spring.

LEFT: Blossom is the highlight of many spring gardens, with the flowering cherry (Prunus sp.) being one of the best-known and best-loved blossom trees. There are many ornamental flowering cherries, including Cheal's weeping cherry (Prunus serrulata 'Kiku Shidare') which has pendulous branches of deep pink flowers and this shapely white weeping cherry (Prunus serrulata) which can be grown as either a feature or as an accent plant.

No discussion of spring gardening can pass without mention of all the wonderful crab apples (*Malus* species) in flower. These deciduous beauties give a spectacular display of flowers followed by small fruits which can be used for making preserves. Flowers are white or pink to wine-red in color, with more than one hue on each tree. This blend of colors creates a light, shimmering effect. In a small garden, plant *Malus x purpurea* 'Aldenhamensis', which has wine-red flowers followed by purple-red fruits, or *M.* 'Gorgeous', which has pink buds opening to fragrant white flowers. In more spacious gardens choose *M. pumila* (ruby-red flowers fading with age) and *M. yunnanensis* (white or pale pink flowers followed by red fruits, spotted with white).

In terms of pure show, the magnolia family cannot be surpassed—from the compact *M. stellata* (star magnolia),

LEFT: The spectacular flowers of the deciduous Magnolia x soulangeana *appear in early spring; pink-purple on the outside and pure white inside, followed by large, oval leaves. This outstanding hybrid magnolia is a cross between* Magnolia denudata *and* Magnolia liliiflora, *and needs to be planted with some protection against strong winds, which will spoil the flowering effect.*

RIGHT: In late winter and early spring camellias come into their own, filling the garden with glorious blooms. Water well during the flowering period, especially if the weather becomes warm, and feed lightly to encourage new foliage growth. Some varieties benefit from a light pruning to maintain a more dense, shrubby growth habit.

which has a dense, rounded shape and fragrant white flowers, to the powerful *M. x soulangeana,* with its huge cup-shaped blooms of white tinged with purple and pink. On a warm spring day the fragrance of magnolias in the garden can be quite overpowering.

Towards the end of winter, and into early spring, many camellias begin to flower. The white and pale pink varieties need a little more shelter, and should be protected from the morning sun which can burn the petals. The beauty of the camellia—quite apart from the show of flowers—is the solid mass of deep green, glossy foliage that it gives to the garden. There are so many varieties and flower forms to choose from, from the simple single forms such as *C. hiemalis* and *C. cuspidata* to the semi-double, anemone-form, peony-form, rose-form and formal double form. Among my favorites are *C.* 'Guilio Nuccio', which has very large coral-red semi-double flowers; *C.* 'Margaret Davis', which has peony-form flowers of white flushed with rose pink, and *C.* 'William Hertrich', which has semi-double cherry-red blooms. All camellias like moderately rich, well-drained neutral to acid soil, and some of the small varieties can be cultivated with great success in a large container.

Other Spring Beauties

Azaleas (rhododendron species) in all their forms are among the most valued flowering shrubs for the garden. There is an enormous range of flower forms and varieties, blooming from late winter through mid-summer. There are many ways that this group can be used effectively: the larger varieties make wonderful hedges and windbreaks, and azaleas can be used as feature plants, accent plants, in massed plantings or in containers in courtyards or on balconies. The flower colors range from purest white through every shade of pink, red, coral and mauve to purple. I simply adore the mollis azalea, the deciduous form with flowers in the yellow, coral and orange color spectrum. Grouped in a mixed mass planting, it resembles a fruit salad, colorful yet subtle.

In more temperate climates roses will start flowering towards the end of spring, but most will experience recurrent flowering through summer and into autumn or a second flowering period in late summer. Many of the old-fashioned favorites will have one dramatic flush of flowers and this should be a consideration when choosing varieties for specific purposes. Roses will be dealt with in more detail in Chapter 6, 'The Garden in Summer'.

Spring-flowering climbers include *Jasminum polyanthum* (jasmine), which will fill the garden with fragrance; *Beaumontia grandiflora* (herald's trumpet), which is a vigorous twining climber with large white flowers; *Stephanotis floribunda* (Madagascar jasmine), with its scented, waxy white flowers; and all the early-flowering clematis. *Clematis aristata* gives a stunning display of white starry flowers in mid-spring, and the well-known and much-loved *C. montana* is also a prolific flower producer if planted against a sunny wall or pergola. *C. montana* var. *rubens* is the pink form. Clematis appreciates a bit of pruning back after flowering, to encourage new growth to ripen for the next season. It looks wonderful intertwined with other climbers, such as *Rosa banksia*, to produce a heady tangle of flowers and fragrance.

LEFT: Forget-me-nots (Myosotis sp.) *are among the best ground-covering annuals, self-seeding and popping up all over the garden season-after-season. Indeed they can be a pest if allowed to seed too readily, with young plants overwhelming other, more sensitive, species. Here they form a pretty carpet around red and yellow tulips* (Tulipa sp.)*, with their bright blue flowers providing a great color contrast.*

THE
GARDEN IN
SUMMER

The Busy Garden

As the summer days grow longer the garden takes on an entirely new atmosphere. Blossom trees have dropped their flowers and are now clothed in handsome fresh foliage; most of the spring bulbs have died back, and spring-planted annuals are starting to mature. The garden is alive with bird and insect life, and the delicate balance of nature between plant and insect life should be apparent. Far too many gardeners wage a constant battle against

LEFT: As the days grow warmer the garden seems to burst with color and energy, as perennials and spring-planted annuals come into flower. In this mixed bed they have been mingled with rockery and alpine plants, all quite low-growing, to allow a broad display of color. Low stone walls are partially covered by cascading species, and the color range is deliberately bright and varied.

PREVIOUS PAGE: The brilliant contrast of bright yellow yarrow (Achillea taygetea) *and cerise cranesbill* (Geranium palmatum) *makes a strong statement in a lightly shaded corner of a perennial border. The intensity of the color is emphasized by the shadiness of the location — in full sun these same blooms may not appear as vivid, and therefore the contrast will not be as effective.*

insects without realizing that they are all part of nature's plan. It is only when the balance is tipped that a particular insect becomes a 'pest', and requires attention.

Only now are we looking back to how our forebears coped with common problems, in an endeavor to reduce the quantity of chemical sprays and fertilizers poured onto the soil and into the air. Biological control is a very effective way of keeping insects in check. By introducing nectar-producing trees and shrubs, we automatically attract birds to the garden. These birds will forage widely, reducing the insect population on their rounds. Organic gardeners have known for years that chickens scratching in the orchard will reduce fruit fly and other problems that plague fruiting trees. Ducks, too, have a role to play in eliminating snails and slugs that destroy so much new growth. If we don't spray routinely, creatures like the pretty ladybug will return to the garden, devouring aphids with relish.

Taking up this 'alternative' attitude does not mean allowing your favorite roses to become infested with aphids or black spot. One of the hallmarks of a successful organic gardener is constant checking of plants to detect problems

early, before they get out of hand. As you wander through the garden, turn leaves back and check the undersides—this is where problems so often occur. When hand watering look closely at each plant, as this regular contact will keep you in touch with the general health of the garden. Many sap-sucking insects can simply be removed manually, or hosed away. Affected foliage can be removed and burnt. Remedial action taken early will save heartache at a later stage.

Be aware also that the health of the garden will greatly depend on the condition of the soil. In summer the garden can easily dry out, especially in warmer regions that experience a lower natural rainfall. When plants are stressed by heat and by dryness they will be far more susceptible to insect attack and various diseases. So use summer as a time to keep the garden thriving, by routine watering in those areas that experience insufficient rainfall, and by mulching the soil surface with organic matter (composts, and manures) to keep weed growth down and prevent the soil from drying out. Hot winds, in particular, can cause a lot of damage, and the gardener must be prepared to water regularly.

Warm Days of Roses

There is so much activity in the summer, and there are so many wonderful plants to enjoy. Roses suddenly come into their own: old-fashioned moss and cabbage roses, wild roses with their simple five-petal formation, and the unforgettable climbers and ramblers. Against the back wall of my garden I have a relatively young 'New Dawn', which constantly enchants me with its coverage of pale pink flowers. I also have a 'Mermaid', a vigorous climber, and I suspect I will have to move it at some stage because it threatens to take over the trellis area of the garden. The clear yellow blooms are quite magical in the late afternoon, after the

LEFT: Glorious climbing roses cover a sturdy log pergola, strong enough to support their weight even when mature. Climbers are particularly hardy and fast-growing; here Rosa *'Wedding Day' (white flowers),* Rosa *'Bleu Magenta' (rich purple flowers) and* Rosa *'Bantry Bay' (deep pink flowers) have been selected to eventually intertwine, forming a halo of mixed colors.*

garden has been watered. Last year it continued to flower well into late autumn, with buds still appearing in the early weeks of winter.

Other yellow climbers of note include 'Lawrence Johnston', a vigorous grower with butter yellow blooms; the less invasive 'Le Rêve', a hybrid form of *Rosa foetida*; and 'Easlea's Golden Rambler', which produces glorious clusters of fully double, apricot-yellow flowers. These make wonderful cut flowers for the house. Climbers have so many uses: to hide unsightly fences or gates, to cover a trellis or pergola, or to form a colorful rose arch that will frame another view of the garden. The traditional rose arch can be placed at the gate to welcome visitors to the garden, or can span a gently curved pathway that leads from one area of the garden to another.

The most disconcerting aspect of growing roses is deciding which cultivar to plant, as there are literally thousands to choose from. Each year new hybrids are introduced—shrubs, floribundas and hybrid teas—to the point where deciding what to grow becomes overwhelmingly

confusing. Add to this number all the old varieties that have been reintroduced, prized for their soft stems, flowers and heady fragrance. My advice is to see what other people are growing, and select the ones you most admire. Among my personal favourites are 'Complicata', which is a vigorous Gallica rose with fragrant single flowers of pink with pale centers; 'Boule de Neige', a charming Bourbon rose with fully double, white flowers (sometimes tinged with pink) with a wonderful fragrance; and 'Henri Martin', which is a crimson moss rose that grows vigorously and has stems covered with the characteristic 'mossing'.

During summer I pick roses daily, to encourage more blooms, and to enjoy them in the house as well as in the garden. For those who prefer not to prune roses too hard, set aside a bed that can be an informal planting, where roses can be allowed to spread at will. Climbers can be established at the foot of mature trees and allowed to shoot upwards. Don't attempt to match a vigorous rose with a sensitive tree, or the latter will quickly be overwhelmed!

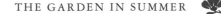

Perennials and Bright Flowers

Summer is truly the time for perennials, and many come into their own from late spring onwards: campanulas, verbenas, tall spikes of lupines, massed groupings of geranium (cranesbill), phlox, astilbe, acanthus, linaria, salvia and chrysanthemums. Artemesias, achilleas, cinerarias and verbascums (mulleins) will be splendid at this time of year. Again, the choice for the gardener is overwhelming. Many perennials are sold as bare-rooted plants in late autumn, and can be heeled-in until spring when they must be positioned where they are to grow. Keeping them in one warm bed during winter prevents them from getting 'lost', and means that they can be tended carefully until the warmer weather arrives. Make sure that the labels are nearby for easy identification, as many are difficult to distinguish before their foliage emerges properly.

Self-seeding perennials such as *Aquilegia vulgaris* (columbines) should be starting to flower now. They are one of the prettiest of all perennial types, with rounded gray-green foliage and spikes of funnel-shaped flowers that range from pink to crimson, purple and white. They will spring, mixing in with the more spectacular hybrid varieties that don't self-seed. A massed planting is a wonderful sight.

Oriental poppies (*Papaver orientale*), with their huge vermilion flowerheads, will start to flower now. All poppies, including the annual variety, are outstanding in beds and borders. The range of flower colors is endless, and it must surely be the slender stems and delicate cup-shaped blooms that catch the eye. No garden is complete without poppies.

Named after the Greek goddess of the rainbow, the *Iris* species will flower from late spring onwards, depending on the variety. There are many divisions in the iris family, and they are classified by their distinctive features and cultural requirements. Among the easiest to grow are the bearded or German irises, although other groups that are popular include evansia (crested) irises, xiphium irises, including the Spanish varieties, and the dwarf reticulata irises. Irises look wonderful in most situations: as clumps in the flower garden; on the water's edge near streams

LEFT: As summer draws to an end brilliant dahlias will come into flower, in a wonderful range of colors and flower forms. The single form, which has eight to ten broad petals, has plenty of old-fashioned charm while those with a more complex flower form have a second 'collar' of smaller petals surrounding an open, central disc. Here warm shades of orange, red and pink have been allowed to cheerfully overlap.

and ponds, and alongside roses. Flower colors range from pure white to many shades of pale blue and pink, violet, lavender and purple, and yellow. Of note is the delightful small *I. innominata,* which grows to only 8 inches in height, with its grassy foliage and flowers of lilac, pale pink or purple according to the variety; *I. graminea,* with its fragrant pink-mauve flowers; and *I. japonica,* which flowers for many weeks with ruffled pale lavender or white blooms.

The lilies of the field, in an amazing array of flower forms and colors, will serve the garden well in summer. There are snowy whites, pinks, reds, yellows and oranges, with many striped, spotted and variegated varieties. There are many plants that carry the name 'lily', but don't actually belong to the genus lilium, and shouldn't be confused. Examples are agapanthus (African lily), amaryllis (Belladonna lily), and crinum (Cape lily). The most popular lilies are the oriental and Asiatic hybrids, with their colorful flowers and lance-shaped foliage. Among the most spectacular are L. 'Journey's End' (bowl-shaped deep pink flowers spotted with maroon), L. 'Bright Star' (flattish white flowers streaked with orange), and the snowy white *L. candidum.*

Dahlias are colorful border flowers, although they have fallen from favor somewhat, as there are more and more interesting and unusual perennials in nurseries these days. Dahlias have many virtues, however, not the least being their ease of cultivation. Staking is often necessary as they come into flower, yet if it is done with care it need not be visible. Flower forms include single, anemone, collarette (single with an inner collar of petals), cactus, pompom and ball-shaped. Colors range from pure white through every shade of pink, red, yellow and orange. I adore the white dahlia 'Snow Elf' (collarette-form) and the brilliant red D. 'Comet' (anemone-form).

Of all the small summer-flowering shrubs, the cistus (rock rose) is probably the most beautiful. Although the flowers are short-lived, they are magnificent. Examples include *C. x aguilari* with its rounded, pure white flowers; *C.* 'Purpureus', which has saucer-shaped deep pink/purple flowers blotched with deep red; and *C.* 'Silver Pink', which has clear-pink blooms with brilliant yellow stamens. Cistus can be grown in difficult areas, on sandy soils and near the seaside. It is also frost-hardy, which makes it adaptable over a wide range of climates.

Mock orange blossom (*Philadelphus coronarius*) is another outstanding summer-flowering shrub, excellent as much for its graceful arching branches as for its fragrant, creamy-white flowers. Mock orange is perfect for the cottage garden, while more formal gardens will benefit from the softness of its outline. It can be planted at the back of a bed or border, or in a massed group for a hedge or screen. It grows to a height of 9 feet, and spreads to about the same width.

RIGHT: Blues and yellows effectively combined in a perennial border of golden yellow yarrow (achillea 'Moonshine'), pale yellow lupins (lupinus 'Russell hybrids'), bright blue spiderwort (tradescantia), and tall blue spikes of bellflowers (campanula). The yellowish-green flowers of lady's mantle (alchemilla) soften the edge of the bed against the pathway.

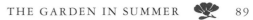

THE
GARDEN IN
AUTUMN

Warm Autumn Hues

The days begin to grow cooler and the garden takes on a mellow look, signaling that autumn has arrived. The remnants of the summer-flowering annuals and perennials are still apparent, and indeed some of these plants will continue to flower for many weeks to come. The garden relaxes as the midday heat loses its fierce intensity. This is particularly noticeable in warmer climates, where the summer sun can make the garden appear bleached out and exhausted; colors seem to return to normal in autumn.

Hollyhocks, tuberous begonias and dahlias are at their best in autumn.

*LEFT: Virginia creeper (*Parthenocissus quinquefolia*) is a self-clinging deciduous climber that is marvelous for covering walls and fences, making a colorful leafy backdrop for beds and borders. It is seen here growing against a stone wall with ivy (*Hedera helix*), with green foliage that makes a wonderful contrast to its vivid red foliage.*

*PREVIOUS PAGE: In autumn the brilliant red foliage of the scarlet oak (*Quercus coccinea*) will last for several weeks, falling to form a carpet of leaves. These leaves can be raked and composted or used as an excellent mulch, especially around azaleas, rhododendrons and other acid-loving species.*

Hollyhocks are beautiful when full grown, although they will often need staking support, especially if the garden bed is windswept. Snails and slugs are drawn to these slow-growing beauties, and it will take vigilance to keep them at bay for the entire growing period. I have been amazed to observe snails suddenly appearing just at flowering time, determined on destruction. Some varieties of dahlia, too, need to be staked and protected from slugs. Dahlias are quite heavy feeders, and do best if fed routinely during summer.

Many roses will still be flowering in autumn, and bushes should be fed to maintain good flower production. Don't add any mulch as the weather cools, as this will prevent the soil from getting warm on the cold days of autumn and winter. By all means tidy up rose bushes as they near the end of the flowering period, but don't prune them now or they will begin new growth, which will only be damaged by late winter frosts.

Towards the middle of autumn the soil can be enriched with organic matter in preparation for the planting of spring-flowering annuals, bulbs and perennials. Tulips, daffodils, jonquils, snowdrops, freesias and hyacinths can all be planted now, and good drainage is vital if they are to give the desired display in spring. Some gardeners add a scoop of clean river sand to the base of the planting hole to improve drainage conditions. Raised beds will also help. Bulbs can be bought in bulk for naturalizing at the base of deciduous trees. This is backbreaking work, but the rewards are tangible. In autumn I plant seeds and seedlings of aquilegias, foxgloves, poppies, lupines and primulas, in every available spot between the perennials, which will die back in winter.

Red and orange foliage on trees is the most noticeable indication that autumn has arrived. This brilliant flash of color is much more vivid in cool to cold climates, although some change can be witnessed in warmer regions. Large gardens can be ablaze with maples (*Acer* species) and oaks (*Quercus* species), while the lofty *Liquidamber styraciflua* (sweet gum) is also suitable for more spacious areas. Planted in groves or as a woodland grouping, it gives a most dramatic display. Maples are excellent trees for medium and small gardens, with dwarf varieties that can be grown successfully in a container. The beautiful *Acer saccharum* (sugar maple) has bright green palmate leaves which turn orange-scarlet as winter approaches, then fall to create a golden carpet. The smaller maples include *A. palmatum* 'Atropurpureum' and *A. palmatum* 'Dissectum', which has low, horizontal growth. The dogwoods (*Cornus* species) are dramatic in autumn, as are *Rhus succedanea* and *R. typhina* with scarlet foliage.

The falling leaves should never be wasted, although they will require raking, which some gardeners loathe. However, as an ingredient of compost, they are a rich annual harvest that must never be ignored. I cringe to see gardeners burning leaves without realizing that they are discarding one of nature's best resources. Leaves can be raked directly onto garden beds as a mulch, or stored separately to slowly break down into 'leaf mulch', which is a valuable soil additive. The leaves of the oak are of particular benefit to plants such as rhododendrons, azaleas and camellias, again used as a direct mulch or dug in later as leaf litter.

One tip is to rake leaves progressively in autumn, rather than waiting until they all fall. If left on the ground too long they will spoil the grass, and become waterlogged, which will make them really hard to gather. A quick tidy-up once or twice a week will make life much easier.

RIGHT: Older stone houses are ideal for covering with Boston ivy (Parthenocissus tricuspidata), *although this fast-growing creeper may need to be controlled if its suckers invade the mortar, sometimes causing it to crumble. The orange and yellow chrysanthemums will flower well into autumn, and can be cut back after flowering, in preparation for the following season.*

Reds, Blues and Yellows

Just as the leaves of trees turn glorious shades of red and orange in autumn, so too do various climbers. *Parthenocissus tricuspidata* (Boston ivy) will give a spectacular crimson display now, covering large expanses of wall or fence. *P. henryana* (Chinese Virginia creeper) has interesting variegated leaves, which remain so when they turn fiery red, while *P. tricuspidata* 'Veitchii' has foliage that deepens to a rich red-purple, and dull blue berries. Don't forget *Vitis coignetiae* (crimson glory vine) and *Vitis vinifera* 'Purpurea' (claret vine), which are vigorous tendril climbers with large leaves that are brightly colored in autumn. These climbers have a multitude of uses, and can be trained to form a canopy of leaves through established trees.

Asters (Michaelmas daisies) are highly prized as autumn-flowering perennials, and there are many varieties from which to choose. *Aster ericoides* 'White Heather' and *A. vimineus* are covered with tiny white flowers, while *A. cordifolius* 'Silver Spray' produces graceful sprays of white blooms tinged with pink or lavender.

A. novi-belgii has larger flowers and cultivars such as *A.* 'Carnival' (double cerise-red flowers) and *A.* 'Marie Ballard' (double mid-blue flowers). *A. novae-angliae* also has a host of cultivars. Although they can be dotted through a flower border, asters also look quite splendid as a massed planting. Several varieties can be grouped together, flowering at once and giving a colorful display. Rich, moist soil is essential for success.

The tall, colorful spikes of the kniphofias (red hot pokers, torch lilies) emerge at this time of year, providing good accents at the back the garden. They can. be grouped together in clumps, or scattered throughout the garden. *Kniphofia* 'Percy's Pride' grows to 3 feet with spikes of creamy flowers tinged with yellow and green; *K. triangularis* has dramatic flame-red flower spikes; while *K. caulescens* has blue-green foliage and salmon-red flower spikes that appear from late summer onwards. *K. uvaria* var. *nobilis* is the variety with brilliant flowers given the common name 'red hot poker'.

LEFT: *Fiery oranges, reds and yellows combine in a brilliant autumnal border, with tall spikes of red hot poker (Kniphofia caulescens) surrounded by dahlias and black-eyed Susan (rudbeckia). There are several valuable species of kniphofia, which is also sometimes called torch lily, and they make a useful addition to borders, providing height, attractive foliage and a tremendous splash of color.*

ABOVE: *Brilliant yellows that enrich the landscape include sneezeweed* (Helenium sp.)*, yarrow* (Achillea sp.) *and* Rudbeckia sp. *Expect flowering from mid-summer well into autumn.*

Some chrysanthemums will continue flowering through autumn, and even later in warmer climates. *Chrysanthemum rubellum* 'Clara Curtis' is a particularly beautiful variety, growing to 2 feet, with a profusion of flat daisy flowers of clear pink with yellow centers. It would look pretty in a massed planting backed by *Aster novae-angliae* 'Harrington's Pink', which has similar flowers but a taller growth habit.

For a splash of yellow in autumn look for *Helianthus x multiflorus*, an upright perennial with large golden flowers with double centers, and H. 'Loddon Gold', which also has vivid deep yellow blooms. Both varieties need staking as they come into flower. The charming rudbeckia 'Herbstsonne' should flower at the same time. Its daisy-like flowers are a warmer yellow, and have conical green centers. At the front of the garden *Arctotheca calendula* (Cape dandelion) will form a carpet of woolly green foliage covered with bright yellow daisy-like flowers with a deeper yellow center. As a blue/purple contrast the Cape dandelion could be mingled with *Aster amellus*, which has violet flowers with yellow centers, or the dainty *Liriope muscari,* which has spikes of rounded bell-shaped flowers against a background of glossy green foliage.

Another favorite for this time of the year is the rose-pink *Sedum spectabile* 'Brilliant', which grows to 1 foot with fleshy gray-green leaves and flat heads of bright flowers. Certain bulbs will now appear, including the nerines with their delicate lily-like flowers. The genus includes *Nerine bowdenii alba*, which has white flowers tinged with pink, and *N. undulata* and *N. bowdenii,* which both have pink flowers. N. 'Orion' is a much larger-flowered variety, again in a soft shade of pink, while N. 'Brian Doe' has blooms in a rich shade of salmon. A most unusual bulb for a warm and sheltered part of the garden is *Haem-anthus coccineus* (blood lily), with its thick spotted stems and tiny red flowers with showy stamens. Cyclamens and crocuses will start to pop from the ground in late autumn and winter, in an amazing range of flower colors. They prefer a cool to cold climate and rich soil if they are really to thrive.

Berries are also in abundance now, mostly red and often very showy. *Euonymus japonicus* (Japanese spindle tree) has green star-shaped flowers followed by pink berries with green seeds; the striking *Crataegus* genus (hawthorns), including *C. x smithiana* and *C. phaenopyrum,* has both red foliage and berries; *Vitex acuminata* has white flowers in autumn, followed by masses of round cherry-red berries; and the malus species (crab apples) also carry yellow or purple fruits, depending on the type, at this time. The genus *Sorbus* also has trees with colored foliage and berries, including *S. commixta* and *S. aucuparia* (mountain ash), which are both laden with orange, red and yellow berries over handsome foliage.

RIGHT: In autumn look for berries, too, in orange, yellow and red tonings. The brilliant orange-red fruits of the firethorn (Pyracantha coccinea) will cover the tree from autumn to winter, following white flowers in summer. There are pure orange and golden-yellow firethorns, and the same colors in cotoneaster berries as well.

THE
GARDEN IN
WINTER

The Winter Sleep

When all the leaves of autumn have been raked, and the shapely outlines of the deciduous trees have been exposed, winter has truly arrived. I enjoy this time of year, but find gardening difficult because the soil is hard, cold and unyielding. Everything slows to a standstill; most insects and pests vanish, the compost seems to stagnate, and growth ceases for most species. In colder climates snow is

LEFT: Lenten roses (Helleborus sp.) are one of the great pleasures of winter, forming clumps of glossy green foliage and producing masses of rich purple, purplish-green or white flowers according to the species. These perennials can be grown in a wide range of conditions, and are excellent for shady parts of the garden where little else will grow. Seen here amid a sea of snowdrops (Galanthus sp.).

PREVIOUS PAGE: Although the garden rarely looks its best in winter, shapes, outlines and textures of plants can be quite dramatic, especially after light snowfall or frost. In cold climate gardens, plants must be selected to withstand these conditions, including conifers such as juniper (Juniperus chinensis 'Kuriwao') and the evergreen hebe, which has several species that can tolerate very cold conditions.

often a feature, and gardening becomes a virtual impossibility. This is not to say that the landscape is entirely devoid of color and interest, however, in warm climates various flowers and berries have their day.

The handsome *Michelia doltsopa* will produce a wonderful display of fragrant white magnolia-like flowers in late winter, against a backdrop of glossy green foliage. *Erythrina sykesii* (coral tree) is a magnificent tree for temperate climates, with attractive scarlet flowers on its bare branches from mid-winter to spring. It can tolerate a certain degree of frost, and is an ideal specimen for coastal areas. The evergreen *Bauhinia variegata* (orchid tree) flowers now and has fragrant magenta or lavender blooms, while the bushy *Dombeya natalensis* (Natal cherry) gives a show of buttercup-like white flowers which are also quite fragrant.

Three interesting trees for winter fruits are *Corynocarpus laevigatus* (karaka), which has orange fruits; *Ilex pedunculosa* (holly), with its striking bright red berries; and *Alphitonia excelsa* (red ash), which has round black fruits. Cotoneasters will fill the garden with birds as they remain in berry during

winter. Although the fruits are reputed to be poisonous, it doesn't seem to dampen the birds' enthusiasm, and they can make quite a mess as they pick their way through every tree.

Another interesting shrub for winter display is *Garrya elliptica* (silk-tassel bush), so named for the elegant gray-green catkins that appear at this time of the year. It is a dense evergreen plant, growing to 18 feet in the right conditions. However, my favorite is the shimmering *Hamamelis japonica* (witchhazel), which is covered with fragrant yellow flowers on slender bare branches. *H. x intermedia* 'Arnold Promise' is an excellent cultivar, with very large, spidery yellow flowers and oval leaves that turn golden before falling in autumn.

Viburnums flower in late winter and continue into spring. *Viburnum tinus* has leathery, deep green leaves and small white blooms that begin as pink buds in winter. *V. x bodnantense* 'Dawn' is an outstanding cultivar, upright in form, with bronze foliage and racemes of deep pink, fragrant flowers. In mild climates it will start flowering in late autumn and continue into spring.

Color Surprises

Many camellias are at their best in the cooler months of winter, producing a wonderful display of flowers against glossy, deep green foliage. Like roses and azaleas, these plants are greatly admired and therefore new varieties and cultivars are constantly being introduced to an eager market. The flower colors are quite varied, from pure white through every shade of pink to red, and there is even a yellow variety. Flower forms range from single to semi-double, anemone-form, peony-form, rose-form and formal double. There are magnificent striped and mottled flowers, from species such as *Camellia japonica* 'Yamato Nishiki' and *C. japonica* 'Iwane'. In some varieties, the stamens are prominent; in others, they are hidden behind folds of

LEFT: Snow-covered ground is often monotonous, saved by glorious splashes of color when bulbs poke through. From mid-winter expect crocus to emerge, flowers first, followed by strap-like foliage. Crocus tommasinanus has slender, funnel-shaped flowers in a variety of colors including violet, lilac and purple, sometimes silver on the outside of the petals.

petals. If good growing conditions are provided, the camellia can become one of the most valuable plants in the garden, with a solid evergreen outline and a rewarding flowering period.

Roses should be pruned in winter, although the later the better in very cool climates. If they are cut back too soon there is a danger of new growth appearing, which can be greatly damaged by late winter frosts or snow. Always use clean, sharp pruning shears and practice restraint, especially with old-fashioned roses, which often need no more than a simple tidy-up.

Some trees and shrubs are admired for their interesting branches in winter. One such example is *Cornus alba* 'Sibirica' (red-barked dogwood), which produces new scarlet shoots in the colder weather. The outline of *Betula pendula* (silver birch) is hard to beat, with its slender mottled trunk of silver and its pendulous, lacy framework of branches. Birches are ideal for creating a copse, where trees of one species are grouped together to emulate a mini-woodland. Those with slender

upright trunks are preferred, and they should be grouped together at random in odd numbers—never in tidy rows, or symmetrically. Underplant the copse with late winter-flowering bulbs such as jonquils or crocus, for a charming effect.

Winter can also be a time of fragrance in the garden, when members of the daphne species come into flower. The evergreen *Daphne odora* will produce heavenly clusters of purple-pink flowers against mid-green foliage. There is also a variegated form, *D. odora* 'Marginata'. The deciduous *D. mezereum* is a handsome shrub with a covering of pink or purple fragrant flowers in winter, against a framework of bare branches.

The cheerful yellow flowers of senecio will bring some relief to the chill of winter. This evergreen twining climber has various forms, including *S. tamoides,* and *S. mikanioides* (German ivy), which is covered with button-shaped fragrant yellow flowers. The vigorous *Jasminum nudiflorum* is another climber that will flower now, with its delicate, gently fragrant starry yellow flowers.

Perennials

Perennials are a bit of a disappointment in winter, with just a few exceptions. Hellebores (Christmas rose, lenten rose) are the most versatile and adaptable plants, growing in deep shade if required, yet producing glorious nodding cup-shaped flowers that can be creamy-white, pink or purple, according to the species. They are most effective in a large group, or in mass plantings, as the flowers are quite subtle and will get lost in an overcrowded bed or border. *Helleborus x sternii* is a particularly exquisite variety, with showy flowers that are palest green, tinged with pink. A perennial worth mentioning for winter is *Anemone blanda*, a smaller version of *A. apennina*, though it flowers much earlier. The blooms are a wonderful deep blue, and there are cultivars with slightly paler flowers as well as white.

African violets (saintpaulia) are winter-flowering too, but in most climates they are too sensitive for outdoor cultivation. In a greenhouse or similar warm, draft-free situation they will bring great joy with their myriad flower colors and forms. Orchids are another group that need to be grown under glass, or in a sheltered porch or veranda. There are two main groups—epiphytes and terrestrials—both adored by collectors.

The showy hippeastrum will flower during the cooler months, featuring an amazing selection of flower colors—from richest red through pinks to white, with many striped and variegated petal forms. These bulbs can look rather stiff and dull unless grouped together in clumps, or mass planted. *Hippeastrum* 'Red Lion' is an outstanding red variety with yellow anthers, while the more delicate H. 'Apple Blossom' has white blooms tinged with pink at the petal tips. The reliable and hardy clivia is another worthwhile bulb, often seen in public parks and gardens but just as versatile at home. *Clivia miniata* is a small-growing variety, reaching 16 inches, with masses of deep green, strap-like leaves and heads of orange-red flowers in autumn and winter.

Towards the end of winter the bulb *Lachenalia glaucina* appears, with fragrant blue or pale lilac flowers. Snowdrops (galanthus) are a real treat at this time, with white nodding flowers tipped at the ends of the petals with a green spot. The more common *G. nivalis* 'Flore Pleno' can be grown in massive clumps, while *G. elwesii* and *G. ikariae* should be positioned where their more unusual white flowers can be enjoyed. Hyacinths will emerge towards the end of winter, as will the pretty lachenalias and scillas. *Lachenalia aloides* 'Quadricolor' has amazing greenish-yellow and orange flowers, while *L. aloides* 'Nelsonii' has bright yellow blooms, tinged with green. *Scilla mischtschenkoana* is a delicate low-growing bulb with pale blue cup-shaped flowers, while *S. siberica* 'Atrocoerulea' is a taller variety with more showy rich blue blooms. Winter aconite (*Eranthis hyemalis*) grows to only 4 inches, but still causes quite a flurry of color interest with its stalkless, brilliant yellow, cup-shaped flowers.

Winter frosts can be a real problem in some areas, especially hard frosts, which can wipe out areas of the garden that are open and exposed. Those who live in vulnerable areas should be well prepared for the eventuality, and more sensitive plants can be protected with stakes and burlap. This can be rather a nuisance, especially for the diligent gardener who feels the need to take the burlap away on warmer days and replace it in the evening.

As the weather warms there is a temptation to relax, but beware of a late frost, which will destroy newly planted annuals. As spring approaches the color green will simply appear more intense in lawns and mosses. The leaves of *Berberis aquifolium* will begin to color, and the signs will be there for the exciting spring days ahead.

LEFT: Aptly named snowdrops (Galanthus nivalis), *these beautiful bulbs herald the end of winter and the beginning of lush spring growth.*

THE
GARDEN
DIARY

Plants on Record

As the seasons change, the garden offers many surprises, with plants previously hidden beneath the soil surface suddenly emerging from dormancy. Bulbs appear, and flower for a short period, while perennials flower over many months, from spring to autumn, depending on the species.

Often it is hard to recall where certain plants are located when they are dormant, and this is especially true of bulbs, which are often overplanted with annuals to provide color later in the season. I have accidentally disturbed a clump of bulbs

LEFT: Most of the flowers in a typical perennial border can be gathered and pressed, retaining their color and beauty throughout the process. Plants with very fleshy petals, such as lilies, may be difficult to work with, and absorbent paper should be used to take up some of their moisture. After pressing, flowers can be mounted in a frame, or kept in a pressed-flower diary as a record of the garden.

PREVIOUS PAGE: When keeping a photographic record of the garden make sure that each print is labeled with the date, to indicate what is in flower that particular week or month. This is very useful for keeping track of bulbs and perennials which disappear into the ground, and can be easily dug up by mistake. Over several years it is fascinating to observe how the flowering times vary, according to the weather conditions.

when planting annuals and perennials in autumn, and, while this isn't necessarily a disaster, it can be annoying if the bulbs are damaged by the trowel.

Likewise, many perennials disappear from sight in winter, and are forgotten until they reappear in spring. One year I sent away for a large number of mail-order perennials, which arrived in winter when the ground was very cold. I planted them in haste, keeping their identification labels next to each plant. Several weeks later I decided to allow my chickens to scratch through the garden; they are excellent for insect control. They attacked the freshly planted perennials with a vengeance, digging around their roots in search of worms and mites. Although only a few plants were lost, all the labels were displaced and I hadn't a clue which plants were located in which bed. The point of the story is that it is very easy to lose plants, and also to forget their identity once they are planted, especially species that you have never grown before.

Over the years I have developed several ways of keeping track of plants, and methods of teaching myself species identification. The most thorough method is to keep a ground plan, and to mark on it where each plant is located. Ideally, this plan should be drawn to scale, with the main features of the garden, such as paths and garden beds, marked accurately. When a new plant is added it can also be marked on the plan, with a number showing the exact position, corresponding to a key that lists the botanical and common names of each plant, and the date on which it was planted.

Use graph paper for the ground plan, and a pencil for all the notations. This means that the plan can be constantly updated and revised. Active gardeners frequently move plants from one bed to another to achieve a better effect, and these transplants can easily be marked on the graph paper. Sometimes plants die, or simply outlive their beauty or usefulness; they can be removed from the plan easily with an eraser. I often decide to enlarge garden beds, to allow more cultivation space. These major structural changes can also be noted on the ground plan. As you become more familiar with plants, the graph is useful for grouping varieties together according to their requirements and visual compatibility.

Most plants are sold with identification labels, and these can often be left on the plant for a while to jog your memory. Remember that many botanical gardens and show gardens that are open to the public have labels to help visitors identify and recognize every plant. Perhaps in your own garden the labels can be left for 12 months until plants are well estab-

lished, and you have committed names and locations to memory. Also, it is possible to position labels discreetly so they are not a visual distraction. Moreover, although some more fastidious gardeners believe labels spoil the natural appearance of beds and borders, they certainly are very useful for keeping track of plants and memorizing their names. There are many styles to choose from, including plastic tags that push into the ground, or soft metal labels that attach to plant stems (although this type is not very helpful with bulbs and perennials).

Yet another effective method is to keep a catalog book, into which all labels and tags are pasted as a permanent record. Beside each label, note the exact location of the plant, the date planted, and even the nursery from which it was purchased. This can be a delightful record for you to look back on as the garden evolves, remembering the history of each plant. It is also interesting to see how tastes and fashions in plants change as new hybrids and varieties are developed. I have found this catalog method particularly useful when I have planted a variety from the same group of plants, such as roses. With so many varieties to choose from it is easy enough to forget the name of each plant, and a quick look through the catalog is easier than waiting until flowering time and then searching through reference books.

RIGHT: Once flowering has finished this perfect garden scene will be hard to recall unless some record has been kept of the exact position of perennials and bulbs. A photographic diary will help record the seasons and will act as a reminder of glorious summer during bleak winter dormancy.

Pressed Flowers and Photographs

This season I have started a pressed flower diary of my garden, to maintain a monthly record of every flower that appears. This habit is developing into a delightful hobby, and one that can easily be shared with children. Once a week I gather samples of every flower, always looking for a 'perfect' bloom for pressing. I take great care, when pressing it, to maintain the shape and integrity of the flower. I also include sections of the stem, and some of the more interesting feathery-foliage plants or grasses. I keep a list of all the flowers and foliage gathered, and the date on which they were pressed. Obviously, some plants flower over weeks, or months, yet I still gather and press them each week to demonstrate for just how long they were featured in the garden.

When pressing flowers, I use a good quality wax paper and arrange the flowers with plenty of space between them. I haven't invested in a commercial press,

LEFT: There are many ways in which pressed flowers can be used creatively, to make gift cards, small pictures or even a flower calendar. Incorporate pressed foliage as well, to give form and texture to your creations, using tweezers to handle the smaller and more delicate arrangements. Craft glue is used to fix the flowers in position.

still relying on a pile of heavy books to do the job. The results are more than satisfactory! Initially, I plan to make a small picture from each month's collection, with at least one example of each flower represented. I have also seen some charming calendars made from pressed flowers, with each month giving a glimpse of what can be expected in the garden. Pressing flowers is an absorbing hobby, and a beautiful record of the garden year.

The most accurate record, of course, is the color photograph. Every few weeks I capture the garden on slide or print film, taking a variety of angles and views, including overall garden shots and details of various beds and borders. I have found photographs an ideal way of recording the changes of season, and cheering myself up when the garden is looking bleak in mid-winter. It's reassuring to see just how splendid it will soon look, when the weather warms slightly. Mark on the back of each photograph the date taken, and any relevant botanical notes.

From a purely practical point of view, it is also a good idea to write in your diary when major trees and shrubs are at their peak. This is tremendously useful information when planning the plants that are to be located around them. Over the years I have found it fascinating that the flowering time of various trees can

differ as much as three or four weeks, depending on the severity of the winter. Of course this makes planning difficult, but keep in mind that the flowering of other species will probably also be delayed by very cold conditions. In our area there is always a spring garden festival, when the best gardens are opened to the public to raise money for charity. The organizers dread either unseasonably warm or unseasonably cold winters, as these can mean the gardens are either 'over' or not quite at their peak when the visitors arrive by the busload. Yet there is always something wonderful to see, even if a few of the bulbs have lost their freshness.

Every year I have a small garden party when my magnificent *Magnolia denudata* is in flower, filling the garden with a heady fragrance. With experience I have learned to anticipate the flowering time by the development of the furry buds, and it does vary slightly each year. I always take a photograph, and keep a record of the date of the first flower, and the drop of the last bloom.

While it isn't easy to predict exact flowering times, with care it is possible to coordinate the flowering of compatible plants to give the best display. Your local nursery should be of assistance, giving a guide about the expected flowering times in your particular area.

Planting
Guide

Plants for All Seasons

PLANTS FOR HEDGING

Berberis sp.
Buxus sempervirens (English box)
Chamaecyparis lawsoniana (Lawson cypress)
Cotoneaster simonsii
Cupressocyparis leylandii (Leyland cypress)
Elaeagnus x ebbingei
Erica (heather)
Escallonia
Ilex aquifolium (holly)
Lavandula spica (lavender)
Ligustrum ovalifolium (oval-leaved privet)
Lonicera nitida (shrubby honeysuckle)
Mahonia aquifolium

Osmanthus heterophyllus
Prunus cerasifera
Prunus lusitanica (Portugal laurel)
Pyracantha rogersiana (firethorn)
Rhododendron ponticum
Rosa rugosa hybrids
Santolina chamaecyparissus (cotton lavender)
Tamarix pentandra
Taxus baccata
Thuja plicata (western red cedar)
Tsuga heterophylla (western hemlock)
Viburnum tinus

PLANTS WITH AROMATIC LEAVES

Abies balsamea
Allium tuberosum (garlic chives)
Angelica archangelica
Anthemis lactiflora (camomile)
Artemisia dracunculus (tarragon)
Calamintha nepetoides
Dictamnus albus (gas plant)
Helichrysum augustifium (curry plant)
Hyssopus officinalis (hyssop)
Lavandula spica (lavender)
Monarda didyma (sweet bergamot)

Ocimum basilicum (basil)
Origanum majorana (sweet marjoram)
Pelargonium graveolens (rose geranium)
Pelargorium quercifolium (oak-leaved geranium)
Phacelia campanularia
Rosmarinus officinalis (rosemary)
Satureia hortensis (summer savory)
Satureia montana (winter savory)
Tagetes tenuifolia (marigold)
Thuja plicata
Thymus vulgaris (thyme)

LEFT: For centuries used as an essential ingredient of perfumes, lavender (Lavandula sp.) is also prized for its soft gray-green foliage and pretty purple flower spikes. It can be grown in the herb or flower garden, and makes an ideal plant for container cultivation.

PREVIOUS PAGE: Beautiful purples, Salvia nemorosa and cranesbill (Geranium sp.) work well together, with complementary foliage and flowers. It is often hard to visualize how plants will look when mature, making their placement in the flower border a dilemma. Remember that most can be lifted and moved if they don't work well in a particular position.

PLANTS WITH SILVER-GRAY OR BLUE-GRAY FOLIAGE

Abutilon vitifolium
Achillea (yarrow)
Anaphalis triplinervis (pearly everlasting)
Androsace lanuginosa (rock jasmine)
Anthemis cupaniana
Arctotis x hybrida
Artemisia absinthium 'Lambrook Silver' (wormwood)
Artemisia arborescens (wormwood)
Artemisia schmidtiana 'Nana'
Buddleia fallowiana 'Alba'
Cedrus atlantica glauca (blue cedar)
Centaurea gymnocarpa
Cerastium tomentosum (snow in summer)
Convolvulus cneorum
Cupressus glabra (Arizona cypress)
Dianthus (border carnation)
Erica tetralix 'Alba Mollis' (heath)
Eryngium giganteum
Euphorbia wulfenii (spurge)
Helianthemum nummularium (sun rose)
Juniperus communis
Juniperus scopulorum (western red-cedar)
Juniperus squamata 'Meyeri' (juniper)

Lavandula spica
Lychnis coronaria (rose campion)
Lychnis flos-jovis 'Hort's Variety' (flower of jove)
Nepeta x faassenii
Onopordum acanthium (cotton thistle)
Origanum majorana
Oxalis adenophylla
Phlomis fruticosa (Jerusalem sage)
Populus alba (white poplar)
Potentilla nitida 'Rubra'
Pyrus salicifolia 'Pendula' (willow leaved pear)
Rananculus gramineus (buttercup)
Raoulia australis
Ruta graveolens 'Jackman's Blue'
Salix lanata (woolly willow)
Sempervivium arachnoideum (cobweb houseleek)
Senecio cineraria 'White Diamond'
Stachyl byzantina (lamb's ears)
Tanacetum haradjanii
Teucrium fruticans
Verbascum bombyciferum (mullein)
Verbascum 'Gainsborough'
Veronica incana (speedwell)

FLOWERS AND GRASSES FOR CUTTING AND DRYING

Achillea sp. (yarrow)
Agrostis nebulosa (cloud grass)
Anaphalis yedonsis (pearly everlasting)
Briza maxima (pearl grass)
Catananche caerulea (cupid's dart)
Centaurea dealbata
Centaurea macrocephala
Cortaderia selloana (pampas grass)
Didiscus caeruleus (blue lace flower)
Eremurus bungei (foxtail lily)

Gypsophila paniculata
Hordeum jabatum (squirrel-tail grass)
Lagurus ovatus (hare's tale grass)
Liatris spicata (gayfeather)
Limonium sinuatum (statice)
Pennisetum orientale
Scabiosa atropurpurea
Stipa pennata (feather grass)
Tricholaena rosea (ruby grass)
Xeranthemum annuum (everlasting flower)

TOP: Here the silver-gray new growth of lamb's ears (Stachys byzantina) *makes even more dramatic the brilliant red petals of the tulips.*

BOTTOM LEFT: Silver foliage plants create a wonderful color contrast in beds and borders, accentuating the beauty of other species. One of the easiest to cultivate is lamb's ears (Stachys byzantina), *a perennial that quickly spreads to form a large clump of soft gray growth.*

BOTTOM RIGHT: Lilacs (Syringa sp.) *are valued for their huge panicles of fragrant flowers, which vary in color from pure white through lilac to deep purple.*

ABOVE: The fragrance of the rose has often been sacrificed in modern hybridization, although the magnificent rosa 'Mr. Lincoln' has retained a rich perfume as well as a perfect rich red flower form.

RIGHT: Variegated foliage such as the Cornelian cherry (Cornus mas 'Elegantissima') is often used to lighten and brighten a garden scene, especially those species with green and cream leaf combinations.

PLANTS WITH FRAGRANT FLOWERS

Abelia chinensis
Acacia dealbata (wattle)
Boronia heterophylla
Boronia serrulata
Brachycome iberidifolia (swan river daisy)
Buddleia alternifolia
Carpentaria californica
Cestrum nocturnum
Cheiranthus cheiri (wallflower)
Choisya ternata
Chrysanthemum rubellum
Clematis recta
Crinum sp.
Cytisus battandieri (broom)
Daphne sp.
Datura candida
Dianthus sp. (carnations, pinks)
Freesia sp.
Galtonia candicans
Gardenia jasminoides
Heliotropium peruvianum
Hoya carnosa
Hyacinthus sp. (hyacinth)
Jasminum sp.
Lathyrus odoratus (sweet pea)
Lavandula spica (lavender)
Lilium candidum (madonna lily)
Lilium regale
Magnolia grandiflora
Michelia figo
Muscari (grape hyacinth)
Narcissus (jonquil)
Petunia x hybrida
Philadelphus sp. (mock orange)
Phlox maculata
Plumaria (frangipani)
Reseda odorata (mignonette)
Robinia pseudoacaca
Rosa sp. (numerous varieties)
Syringa vulgaris (lilac)
Tulipa sp. (tulips)
Viburnum sp.
Wisteria sinensis (Chinese wisteria)

PLANTS WITH VARIEGATED FOLIAGE

Acer negundo 'Variegatum' (box elder)
Acer platanoides 'Drummondii' (Norway maple)
Actinidia kolomikta
Ajuga reptans 'Variegata'
Amaranthus tricolor
Arum italicum 'Pictum'
Buxus sempervirens 'Aureovariegata'
Cyclamen cilicium
Cyclamen repandum
Daphne odora 'Aureomarginata'
Elaeagnus pungens 'Maculata'
Euonymus fortunei 'Silver Queen'
Euonymus japonicus 'Ovatus aureus'
Euphorbia marginata (snow on the mountain)
Hedera canariensis 'Variegata' (ivy)
Hedera colchica 'Dentata-Variegata' (ivy)
Hedera helix 'Glacier' (ivy)
Hosta crispula (plantain lily)
Hosta fortunei 'Albopicta' (plantain lily)
Hosta undulata (plantain lily)
Humulus scandens
Hypericum x moserianum 'Tricolor'

Ilex aquifolium 'Argentea marginata' (variegated English holly)
Ilex x altaclarensis 'Golden King' (golden variegated holly)
Iris ensata 'variegata'
Iris pallida 'Argenteo-variegata'
Lamium galeobdolon 'Variegatum'
Lamium maculatum 'Roseum'
Lonicera japonica 'Aureoreticulata'
Lunaria annua 'Variegata' (honesty)
Melissa officinalis (golden balm)
Mentha rotundifolia 'Variegata' (apple mint)
Molinia caerulea 'Variegata'
Nymphaea 'Marliacea chromatela'
Pachysandra terminalis 'Variegata'
Pelargonium x hortorum 'Tricolor'
Pieris japonica 'Variegata'
Pulmonaria saccharata (lungwort)
Salvia officinalis 'Tricolor'
Scrophularia aquatica 'Variegata'
Tulipa 'Oriental Splendour' (tulip)
Vinca major 'Variegata' (greater periwinkle)
Weigela florida
Zea mays 'Gracillima Variegata'

PLANTS WITH ORNAMENTAL FRUITS

Abies koreana (Korean fir)
Arbutus unedo (strawberry tree)
Berberis darwinii (barberry)
Callicarpa bodinieri giraldii
Calocedrus decurrens (incense cedar)
Cedrus libani (cedar of Lebanon)
Celastrus orbiculatus
Celastrus scandens (American bittersweet)
Clerodendron
Colutea aborescens (senna)
Cotoneaster sp.
Crataegus x lavallei 'Carrierei' (hawthorn)
Euonymus europaeus 'Red Cascade' (common spindle tree)
Gaultheria procumbens
Geum montanum
Hypericum x inodorum (St John's wort)

Ilex sp. (holly)
Iris foetidissima (Gladwyn iris)
Lunaria annua (honesty)
Mahonia aquifolium
Malus x robusta 'Red Siberian'
Malus 'Golden Hornet' (flowering crab apple)
Malus 'John Downie' (flowering crab apple)
Pernettya mucronata
Physalis franchetii (Chinese lantern)
Rosa moyesii 'Geranium'
Skimmia japonica
Sorbus 'Joseph Rock' (mountain ash)
Symphoricarpos rivularis (snowberry)
Taxus sp.
Viburnum davidii
Viburnum opulus

Index

Photography Credits

Envision/Grace Davies *pp. 68/69*

Garden and Landscape Pictures *p.10* (Mr & Mrs Mann), *p.17* (Lothian Garden, Mrs Woolf), *p.40* (Lothian Garden, Mrs Woolf), *p.60* (Wakehurst Place Garden), *p.98* (The Priory, Kemerton, Mr & the Hon. Mrs Peter Healing), *p.111* (Lothian Garden, Mrs Woolf)

Ivy Hansen Photography *p 77*

Jerry Harpur *p.45* (The Old Rectory, Burghfield), *p.48* (The Old Rectory, Sudborough), *p.52* (Lady Barbirolli)

Insight Picture Library *pp. 116/117*

Jaisay Pty Ltd *p.114*

Andrew Lawson *p.32, p.36, p.92, p.97, p.102, p.106*

Charles Mann Front Cover, Endpapers, *p.4, p.8, p.14* (Chilcombe), *p.19, p.24, p.56* (Madspen House), *pp.12/13, pp.80/81,*

S & O Mathews Back Cover, *pp.20/21, p.27* (Brook Cottage), *p.73, p.121 top*

Mary Moody *p.28, p.29, p.75, p.121 right*

Clive Nichols *pp.2/3, p6/7, p.22* (The Priory), *p.25* (Little Bowden), *pp.30/31* (Chenies), *p.84, p.89, p.95* (Lower House Farm), *pp. 100/101* (The Dingle), *p.104, pp.108/109, p.113* (Helen Dillon's Garden, Dublin), *p.121* left (Lower Severalls), *p.123* (The Anchorage)

Joanne Pavia *p.70, p.79*

Photo/Nats *pp. 90/91*

Harry Smith *p.65, p.82, p.87*

Weldon Publishing *p.5* (Richard Hersey), *p.23, p.76* (Tony Rodd) *p.118, p.122* (Richard Hersey)

Meredith ® Books
President, Book Group: Joseph J. Ward
Vice President and Editorial Director: Elizabeth P. Rice
Executive Editor: Nancy N. Green
Art Director: Ernest Shelton

Published by Lansdowne Publishing Pty Limited,
70 George Street, Sydney, NSW, 2000, Australia.

Project Editor: Deborah Nixon
Designer: Kathie Baxter-Smith
Illustrator: Valerie Price

Meredith Corporation Corporate Officers:
Chairman of the Executive Committee: E.T. Meredith III
Chairman of the Board, President
and Chief Executive Officer: Jack D. Rehm
Group Presidents:
Joseph J. Ward, Books
William T. Kerr, Magazines
Philip A. Jones, Broadcasting
Allen L. Sabbag, Real Estate
Vice Presidents:
Leo R. Armatis, Corporate Relations
Thomas G. Fisher, General Counsel and Secretary
Larry D. Hartsook, Finance
Michael A. Sell, Treasurer
Kathleen J. Zehr, Controller and Assistant Secretary

First Published 1993
by Lansdowne Publishing Pty Limited
First printed in the U.S.A. in 1994
© Copyright Lansdowne Publishing Pty Limited
© Copyright design Lansdowne Publishing Pty Limited

Library of Congress Catalog Card Number: 93-86611
ISBN: 0-696-00099-7

Front cover: The matt-forming Phuopsis *in harmony with cranesbill (*Geranium sp.*)*
*Back cover: Pretty pansies (*Viola sp.*) and tulips (*Tulipa sp.*).*
Title page: The nodding purple flowerheads of Allium aflatunense *and climbing wisteria.*
*Opposite contents page: A winning combination of chives (*Allium schoenproaseum*), sage (*Salvia officinalis*)*
*and everlastings (*Helichrysum italicum*)*
Contents page: The popular mauve-blue blooms of Rosa 'Blue Moon'.
*Endpapers: The deciduous smoke tree (*Cotinus sp.*) growing alongside lungwort (*Pulmonaria sp.*).*